MEDIAEVAL SOURCES
IN TRANSLATION

20

PETER ABELARD

A DIALOGUE OF A PHILOSOPHER
WITH A JEW, AND A CHRISTIAN

Translated by

PIERRE J. PAYER

PONTIFICAL INSTITUTE OF MEDIAEVAL STUDIES

TORONTO, 1979

ACKNOWLEDGMENT

This book has been published with the help of a grant from the Canadian Federation for the Humanities, using funds provided by the Social Sciences and Humanities Research Council of Canada.

CANADIAN CATALOGUING IN PUBLICATION DATA

Abailard, Pierre, 1079-1142.
A dialogue of a philosopher with a Jew, and a Christian

(Mediaeval sources in translation ; 20 ISSN 0316-0874)

Translation of Dialogus inter philosophum, iudaeum et christianum.
Bibliography: p.
Includes index.

ISBN 0-88844-269-6

I. Payer, Pierre J., 1936-   II. Pontifical Institute of Mediaeval Studies.   III. Title.   IV. Series.

B765.A23D63   189'.4   C79-094332-8

PRINTED BY UNIVERSA PRESS, WETTEREN, BELGIUM

To Trudy

Contents

I would like to thank the readers for the Pontifical Institute of Mediaeval Studies, the reader for the Canadian Federation for the Humanities, and Dr. Philip McShane and Dr. Larry Fisk of Mount Saint Vincent University for the care they showed in examining the manuscript and for their invaluable suggestions in regard to items of translation and style.

Introduction

Peter Abelard and his contemporaries were familiar with the division of history into three great periods which reflect the interventions of God in time. Hugh of St. Victor says: "For there are three periods of time through which the space of this world runs. The first is the period of the natural law, the second the period of the written law, the third the period of grace. The first is from Adam even unto Moses, the second from Moses even unto Christ, the third from Christ even unto the end of the world."[1] Hugh goes on to say that there are three kinds of men corresponding to these periods: pagans, Jews, and Christians, and that "these three kinds of men have never been wanting at any time from the beginning."[2] Abelard presents representatives of these three kinds of men in his *Dialogue of a Philosopher with a Jew, and a Christian.* Hugh says that the men of the natural law direct their lives by natural reason alone, but that they walk according to concupiscence and are openly evil.[3]

---

[1] Hugh of St. Victor, *On the Sacraments of the Christian Faith* 1.8.11, tr. Roy J. Deferrari (Cambridge, Mass., 1951), p. 149. This division derives from Augustine, *Faith, Hope, and Charity* 118, tr. L. A. Arand, Ancient Christian Writers, 3 (Westminster, Maryland, 1947), p. 110. And see Hugh of St. Victor, *On the Sacraments of the Christian Faith* 1.8.3, tr. R. Deferrari, p. 143.

[2] Hugh of St. Victor, *On the Sacraments of the Christian Faith* 1.8.11, tr. R. Deferrari, p. 149.

[3] Ibid.

Abelard's Philosopher is, indeed, a man of the natural law who directs his life by natural reason, and while he is prepared to defend that way of life, he says that he is particularly interested in gaining salvation for his soul. This desire leads him to the discussion with a Jew and a Christian in order to test their credal positions against the rule of reason. In Abelard's *Dialogue* there is no suggestion that the pagan Philosopher walks in concupiscence and is openly evil. It would almost seem that Abelard wants to right the balance offset by Hugh's rather negative account of the men of the natural law and of natural reason. It is at least a very different view of the pagan than that offered by his contemporary, Hugh of St. Victor; and it is precisely such diversity and difference of opinion which makes the twelfth century an intriguing period to study.

Since C. H. Haskins published his classic, *The Renaissance of the Twelfth Century* (1927), it has been a commonplace to see in that century one of the major stages in the development of European intellectual life, and in the last fifty years or so many adequate and sometimes excellent editions of philosophical and theological works of the twelfth century have appeared. However, with some notable exceptions such as John of Salisbury's *Metalogicon*, Abelard's *Ethics*, Hugh of St. Victor's *Didascalicon* and *On the Sacraments of the Christian Faith*, many of these works have not been accessible to interested students and nonspecialists who do not read Latin. It is primarily for these readers that the following work of Abelard has been translated.[4]

---

[4] Details of the above mentioned works can be found in the bibliography. One significant early author of this period has been relatively well served by translators, viz. St. Anselm of Canterbury who died in 1109.

ABELARD

Peter Abelard played a significant role in the development of thought in the first half of the twelfth century. To the general reading public he is known through his poignant and tragic love for Heloise which is recorded in their correspondence and has been celebrated through the ages in fiction and nonfiction alike. His works in logic, ethics, and theology establish him securely in the histories of philosophy and Christian theology. Born in 1079 in Le Pallet, Britanny, his life developed and was formed around a series of conflicts and confrontations, the earliest of which Abelard himself recounted in his autobiographical letter entitled, *History of My Troubles*. His continuing relationship with Heloise after they both entered monastic life is recorded in a series of letters which have been recently translated. The final and perhaps most dramatic confrontation was surely with St. Bernard of Clairvaux which came to a climax at the Synod of Sens in June 1140 when several propositions, allegedly taken from the works of Abelard, were condemned.[5]

---

[5] See J. T. Muckle, *The Story of Abelard's Adversities*. A translation with notes of the *Historia calamitatum* (Toronto, 1954); Betty Radice, tr., *The Letters of Abelard and Heloise* (Penguin Books, 1974). It should be noted here that the authenticity both of Abelard's *History of My Troubles* and of the correspondence between Abelard and Heloise has been and continues to be questioned. For a convenient summary of the history of the dispute regarding the authenticity of the correspondence see, J. Monfrin, "Le problème de l'authenticité de la correspondance d'Abélard et Héloïse," in *Pierre Abélard – Pierre le Vénérable. Les courants philosophiques, littéraires et artistiques en Occident au milieu du XIIe siècle*, ed. by René Louis, Colloques internationaux du Centre national de la recherche scientifique, no. 546 (Paris, 1975), pp. 409-425; for one of the more recent contributions to the discussion see, John F. Benton, "Fraud, Fiction and Borrowing in the Correspondence of Abelard and Heloise," in *Pierre Abélard – Pierre le*

4   INTRODUCTION

Before the actual condemnation Abelard appealed his position
to the pope and set out for Rome to plead his case in person at
the papal court. While at the monastery of Cluny in southern
France, however, Abelard received word that Pope Innocent II
had condemned him as a heretic along with his works and had
forbidden him to teach. Disheartened, Abelard remained at
Cluny whose famous abbot, Peter the Venerable, gave him
refuge and arranged for a meeting of reconciliation between
Bernard and himself. Peter the Venerable seems also to have
effected a reconciliation between Abelard and the pope.[6]
Abelard spent his last years apparently in peace at Cluny and
the sister house of Saint Marcel where he died in 1142.[7]

Vénérable, ed. by R. Louis, 469-506; and John F. Benton and Fiorella
Prosperetti Ercoli, "The Style of the *Historia calamitatum*: A Preliminary
Test of the Authenticity of the Correspondence Attributed to Abelard and
Heloise," *Viator* 6 (1975) 59-86. Some idea of St. Bernard's criticism of
Abelard can be found in Bernard's letter to Pope Innocent II, Letter 190,
which is translated in A. J. Luddy, *The Case of Peter Abelard* (Westminster,
Maryland, 1947), pp. 58-94. For the condemnation of Abelard as a heretic by
Innocent II, see Innocent II, Letters 447 and 448 (PL 179: 515-517). For an
English biography of Abelard see, J. G. Sikes, *Peter Abailard* (Cambridge,
1932).

[6] See B. Radice, *The Letters*, p. 275 for the letter of Peter the Venerable
to Pope Innocent II recounting the reconciliation with Bernard and asking
that Abelard be granted permission to remain at Cluny; see also ed. Giles
Constable, *The Letters of Peter the Venerable* (Cambridge, Mass., 1967), vol.
2, letter 98 (to Innocent II) and letter 168 (to Heloise).

[7] For the possibility of 1144 see E. Buytaert in CC.CM 11: xii. This
volume contains an English introduction to the life and works of Abelard in
which the editor proposes a chronological listing of the works. J. F. Benton
suggests that the date of Abelard's death may very well have been 21 April
1143, "Philology's Search for Abelard in the *Metamorphosis Goliae*,"
Speculum 50 (1975) 216-217.

Abelard was a prolific writer, although he seems to have had trouble finishing his works.[8] Among the works he has left us is a short dialogue in which he recounts a confrontation between a Philosopher and a Jew and between the same Philosopher and a Christian. This *Dialogue* has not received the attention it deserves from scholars and only recently has it been critically edited.[9] There is some controversy surrounding several aspects of the work and while this is not the place to attempt their resolution, perhaps a word is not out of order.

TITLE

We do not have an original title for this work which has been traditionally called, *A Dialogue of a Philosopher with a Jew, and a Christian.* This title is an expansion of the first word of the inscription which one of the manuscripts carries (*Dialogus Petri Baiolardi*) and it is this manuscript which has been the one transcribed in the older editions of the work.[10]

---

[8] "It would seem that two causes contributed to the literary decline of Abelard. An internal cause: his inability to bring a book to completion. An external cause: the rapid speed at which more comprehensive and better organized books appeared on the market." N. Häring, "Abelard Yesterday and Today," in *Pierre Abélard – Pierre le Vénérable.* ed. by R. Louis, p. 355. This article by Fr. Häring is a fascinating account of the fate of Abelard's writings in his own day and of their editorial history up to the present; see p. 370 for the *Dialogue* in particular.

[9] Most recent edition of the *Dialogue*: *Petrus Abaelardus. Dialogus inter Philosophum, Iudaeum et Christianum.* Textkritisch Edition von Rudolf Thomas (Stuttgart-Bad Cannstatt, 1970).

[10] The manuscript is Vienna, Österreichische Nationalbibliothek MS 819, fols. 1r-59v (probably 12th century).

Abelard himself refers to the work in a later commentary on the first two chapters of Genesis (*In Hexaemeron*). The reference is to a second *collatio* (conference) on the supreme good in which, Abelard says, the reader will find an adequate study of the nature of the absolute good, evil, and the indifferent.[11] Although the contemporary editor of the theological works of Abelard understands this reference to be a reference to a title, he does not substantiate this interpretation.[12] The reference by Abelard perhaps explains the additions which a later manuscript of the *Dialogue* makes to the work, e.g., "The preface to the conferences of Peter Abelard begins."[13] I use the traditional title since it most clearly describes the literary structure of the work which in fact comprises two dialogues.

DATE

A second and perhaps more serious controversy surrounds the date of the *Dialogue*. Traditionally it has been believed that the *Dialogue* was one of the last works of Abelard which he wrote at Cluny and which death caused to remain unfinished.

---

[11] See Abelard, *Expositio in Hexaemeron* (PL 178: 768B).

[12] "I prefer to call the work *Collationes* because this seems to be the title which Abelard had in mind ...": E. Buytaert, "Abelard's *Collationes*," *Antonianum* 44 (1969) 18, n. 1. However, it is possible that when he refers to his second conference (*collatio*) Abelard is referring to a division of the work without his mentioning a title. The participants themselves in the *Dialogue* describe the situation as a conference (*collatio*), a meeting (*congressus*), an altercation (*altercatio*), a fight (*pugna*), a disputation (*disputatio*), and a conflict (*conflictus*).

[13] This is Oxford, Balliol College MS 296, fols. 161r-189v (14th century).

Buytaert, however, has argued persuasively that it must be placed earlier than this time, certainly before the Synod of Sens, sometime between 1136 and 1139, and he himself opts for the earlier date of 1136.[14] The dating is important because if the *Dialogue* was not written by Abelard at Cluny in his last days, then those who use these assumed facts to explain its unfinished state and who claim that Abelard modeled his Philosopher on an Arab he learned about from Peter the Venerable while at Cluny, have to look elsewhere for support for their views. If Buytaert is correct then this claim, which was first made by Jolivet, is open to serious question.[15] And if the work is unfinished this would need no further explanation beyond the fact that it was written by an author who left many of his other works unfinished.

It has been suggested that the *Dialogue* is a second installment of an *apologia pro vita sua* by Abelard which he had begun in his *History of My Troubles*.[16] If the work had been

[14] See E. Buytaert, "Abelard's *Collationes*," 33-38. Recently R. Thomas has defended the view that Abelard wrote the *Dialogue* during his last years while at Cluny; see "Die Persönlichkeit Peter Abaelards im *Dialogus inter Philosophum, Iudaeum et Christianum* und in den *Epistolae* des Petrus Venerabilis: Widerspruch oder Übereinstimmung?" in *Pierre Abélard – Pierre le Vénérable*, ed. by R. Louis, pp. 256-260.

[15] See Jean Jolivet, "Abélard et le philosophe (Occident et Islam au xiie siècle)," *Revue de l'histoire des religions* 164 (1963) 181-189.

[16] See H. Liebeschütz, "The Significance of Judaism in Peter Abaelard's *Dialogus*," *Journal of Jewish Studies* 12 (1961) 15-16, and D. E. Luscombe, *Peter Abelard's 'Ethics'*, an edition with introduction, English translation and notes (Oxford, 1971), p. xxvi, although Luscombe admits that it is more than a *pièce justificative*. Note a slight error in Luscombe, p. xxvi, where he says that Abelard was the only one the participants in the *Dialogue* could find who did not belong to one of the three religious schools of thought. Actually the *Dialogue* makes it clear that Abelard was chosen in spite of the

written at Cluny after the Synod of Sens, perhaps some
justification could be made for such a position. However, if it
was written before this time, probably just when Abelard
began his final teaching period at Paris in the last half of the
1130s, it is difficult to understand why an *apologia* should have
been written so soon after the *History of My Troubles* (1132). It
is true that Abelard has the Philosopher praise him for his
knowledge in extravagant terms in the Preface to the *Dialogue*,
and this might be related to a desire to justify himself when he
was facing the new troubles which were arising and which
would lead to the Synod of Sens. However, it can also be
explained by the fact that Abelard seems to have had a rather
good opinion of himself which he did not hesitate to broadcast.
It is hardly enough to justify seeing the work as an apology for
his life to that date.[17]

ANTI-JEWISH?

Although no good study of the *Dialogue* exists in English
and these introductory remarks are not meant to provide such
a study, I believe it is important to point out what the *Dialogue*
is not. From the beginning of Christianity, Judaism has posed

---

fact that he belonged to one of the three religious schools of thought. And see
D. E. Luscombe, "The *Ethics* of Abelard: Some Further Considerations," in
Peter Abelard, ed. by E. Buytaert, Proccedings of the International
Conference, Mediaevalia Lovaniensia, Series I/Studia II (Louvain, 1974),
p. 72.

[17] The praise is given to justify the choice of Abelard by the participants
in the *Dialogue*. A similar technique is used in the introduction to his
Theologia 'Scholarium' where Abelard says that he was asked to write such
a work because of his broad learning, CC.CM 12: 401 (PL 178: 979).

serious problems to the Christian Church and the Church seems to have kept up a constant argument with Judaism from St. Paul's day to very recently. The argument, as we know, has not always been courteous nor has it always remained a battle merely of words.[18] The *Dialogue* of Abelard, in spite of its title and apparent similarity to earlier polemical works, does not belong to this genre of anti-Jewish literature.[19] The presence

[18] In English see A. L. Williams, *'Adversus Judaeos'. A Bird's-Eye View of Christian 'Apologiae' until the Renaissance* (Cambridge, 1935). More recently, see the works of B. Blumenkranz, particularly, *Les auteurs chrétiens latins du moyen âge sur les Juifs et le judaïsme,* École Pratique des Hautes Études-Sorbonne, Sixième section: Sciences économiques et sociales, Études Juives, 4 (Paris, 1963).

[19] It is difficult to determine whether Abelard drew on his knowledge of contemporary Jewish practice and belief in depicting the Jew of the *Dialogue.* His own recorded contacts with Judaism and his attitude towards the study of Hebrew are summarized in B. Smalley, *The Study of the Bible in the Middle Ages,* 2nd rev. ed., 1952 (Notre Dame, Indiana, 1964), pp. 77-79; and see A. Grabois, "The *Hebraica Veritas* and Jewish-Christian Intellectual Relations in the Twelfth Century," *Speculum* 50 (1975) 617, n. 20. No doubt Abelard would have been aware of Augustine's recommendations regarding the study of Hebrew, *On Christian Doctrine* 2.11, tr. D. W. Robertson Jr., The Library of Liberal Arts (Indianapolis, Indiana, 1958), p. 43. H. Liebeschütz, p. 13, claims that the *Dialogue* shows no influence of traditional Jewish exegesis. E. A. Synan, "The *Exortacio* against Peter Abelard's *Dialogus inter Philosophum, Iudaeum et Christianum,* in *Essays in Honour of Anton Charles Pegis,* ed. by J. R. O'Donnell (Toronto, 1974), p. 179 and n. 9, seems to suggest that there is some echo of the Talmud in the words of the Jew. The suggestion is made that the faith of the Jew comprises his faith in the Hebrew Scriptures "which constitute, along with rabbinic forward defenses, his 'Law'." References to the *Dialogue* are to passages in which the Jew is speaking about the protective function of the legal observances of the Law in sheltering the Jewish people from their neighbors, see below, pp. 47-48. Synan refers to *Aboth* 1.1 which reads: "Moses received the Torah at Sinai and transmitted it to Joshua, Joshua to the Elders, and the Elders to the Prophets, and the Prophets to the men of the great synagogue. The latter

and role of the Philosopher give the work a different orientation and its anti-Jewishness is inspired primarily by rational and not specifically Christian considerations. It is perhaps significant in this regard that in the *Dialogue* there is no confrontation between the Christian and the Jew.

The closest parallel to Abelard's work is perhaps an almost contemporary work by a Spanish Jew, Judah Halevi, entitled *The Kuzari* which was written in 1140.[20] There is a surface similarity between the two which is quite striking. The king of the Khazars relates how in a dream he was drawn to the Jewish religion after hearing the arguments of a philosopher, a Christian scholastic, a Moslem, and finally a rabbi. However, I know of no possible contact nor a common source which might explain what seems to be a coincidental parallel.

---

used to say three things: be patient in [the administration of] justice, rear many disciples and make a fence round the Torah." *The Babylonian Talmud. Seder Nezikin in Four Volumes.* Vol. 4. *Aboth* 1.1, ed. Rabbi I. Epstein (London, 1935), p. 1; see also, *Aboth* 3.13, p. 36 and also *Sanhedrin* in the third volume of the above, p. 303. If the words of the Jew do echo the words of the Talmud, they do not echo its thought in this matter. The Jew of the *Dialogue* is speaking about the prescriptions of the Torah itself while the Talmud speaks about the post-Torah traditions which form a protective fence around the Torah. See Abelard, Sermon 3 (PL 178: 402C-403A). Abelard himself in the Prologue to his *Commentary on the Epistle to the Romans* uses the same idea in justifying the existence of the Epistles in the New Testament in addition to the Gospels; see CC.CM 12: 42.

[20] Judah Halevi, *The Kuzari (Kitab al Khazar)*, translated from the Arabic by Hartwig Hirschfeld, 1905, introduction by Henry S. Slonimsky (New York, 1964). The date is from an internal reference, p. 49. The following came to my attention recently: Aryeh Grabois, "Une chapitre de tolérance intellectuelle dans la société occidentale au XIIᵉ siècle: le *Dialogus* de Pierre Abélard et le *Kuzari* d'Yehudah Halévi," in *Pierre Abélard – Pierre le Vénérable*, ed. by R. Louis, pp. 641-652.

THE DIALOGUE

The author-narrator (Abelard) of the *Dialogue* recounts a dream he had in which a Philosopher, a Jew, and a Christian come to him for help in adjudicating the values of their respective positions. After Abelard agrees to be their judge, the first dialogue between the Philosopher and the Jew begins, comprising about a third of the whole. The second dialogue between the Philosopher and the Christian begins after the Judge is reported to say that he would rather hear the rest of the debate before passing judgment; unfortunately the work ends before the promised judgment is rendered.

In the overall structure of the *Dialogue* Abelard himself is both the author-narrator and a participant. However, he records his own direct discourse participation in the conversation at only one point at the beginning of the work. At the end of the dialogue between the Philosopher and the Jew the remarks of the narrator-judge are reported in indirect discourse and on no other occasion does he actively participate in the *Dialogue*. Given this basic structure, if Abelard's own views are reflected in the work they must be reflected in the views expressed by the other participants. In this regard not enough attention has been paid to the fact that in the first dialogue the Philosopher expresses, sometimes verbatim, views of Abelard himself on the Old Law and its relation to the natural law. Although the parallels are mostly to untranslated works, I have included some of them in the notes. I believe there can be no doubt that the Philosopher is the spokesman for Abelard himself in the discussion with the Jew.

The work itself has no great literary merit as a dialogue because of the extremely long speeches of the participants which are frequently lengthened even more by long citations.[21] On the other hand, the form reflects the contemporary development of the scholastic *quaestio* in which a problem is posed in the form of a question, conflicting solutions are presented, and the discussion is terminated by some professorial opinion.[22] This question form is used in the first dialogue between the Philosopher and the Jew and is more clearly apparent in several exchanges between the Philosopher and the Christian.

I have chosen to translate this work since it draws together so many of Abelard's more interesting and characteristic ideas. In addition, the *Dialogue* contains many early twelfth-century themes which will receive further development throughout the later scholastic period. For these reasons the *Dialogue* is an excellent introduction to the thought of the twelfth-century renaissance.

---

[21] In the midst of a lengthy discourse on the moral virtues the Philosopher says that he must turn his pen (see below, p. 122) to other considerations after the discussion of the virtue of justice. Has the author forgotten he is writing a dialogue? For the same expression see David E. Luscombe, *Peter Abelard's 'Ethics'*, p. 128, and two sermons of Abelard (PL 178: 512c and 582B). These sermons were *written* by Abelard and sent to Heloise (PL 178: 379). However, it is possible that we have here a literary expression which simply refers to a change of topic without connoting a written discourse.

[22] See M. D. Chenu, *Nature, Man, and Society in the Twelfth Century*, selected, edited, and translated by J. Taylor and L. K. Little (Chicago, 1968), pp. 291-298. For an earlier dialogue which reflects an incipient question methodology see Anselm, "Why God Became Man," ed. Eugene R. Fairweather, *A Scholastic Miscellany: Anselm to Ockham*, The Library of Christian Classics, 10 (Toronto, 1970), pp. 100-183.

THE 'EXORTACIO'

Before closing this brief introduction, it should be noted that in the oldest manuscript of the *Dialogue* we possess there is appended to it an *Exortacio magistri ad discipulum de inquisicione summi boni* (*An Exhortation of a Master to a Student concerning the Investigation into the Supreme Good*). The work is a criticism of Abelard's *Dialogue* on the grounds that it does not sufficiently elucidate the nature and location of the supreme good or how one might most directly approach it. This short work has been recently re-edited and prefaced by an explanatory essay.[23]

THE TRANSLATION

A few remarks about the translation:

1. In the main, the following is a translation of the text of the *Dialogue* as edited by Rudolf Thomas, *Petrus Abaelardus. Dialogus inter philosophum, Iudaeum et Christianum* (Stuttgart-Bad Cannstatt, 1970). The advantage of this edition over the one in Migne lies principally in its use of the Oxford, Balliol manuscript which corrects many homoioteleuta and incorporates several significant additions which suggest a later redaction of the work. However, I have also compared the Thomas text with that found in Migne and with the Oxford, Balliol manuscript. Sometimes I corrected the edition, decided against the edition for alternate readings, and I have identified more of the sources used by Abelard. To have annotated all of

---

[23] See E. A. Synan, "The *Exortacio* against Peter Abelard's *Dialogus inter Philosophum, Iudaeum et Christianum*, pp. 176-192.

these variations from the text of Thomas would have been too cumbersome and would serve no useful purpose, and so they have not been noted.

2. The translation of Biblical texts follows *The New American Bible*, by the Confraternity of Christian Doctrine (1970), where possible. Likewise, this version has also been used for the spellings of Biblical names and for the titles of the Books of the Bible.

3. Where English translations of other sources exist I refer to them.

4. Abelard frequently tailors citations of the Bible and of other authors to suit his context, either by omitting phrases or several sentences or by changing the grammar. I have not tried to indicate such omissions or changes but have translated the texts as Abelard presented them.

5. As already noted, I have used the title traditionally given to the *Dialogue*. The introductory headings at the beginning and before each of the dialogues are suggested by the Oxford, Balliol manuscript whose full readings in this regard will be translated in the notes.

6. The notes include some references to Latin works of Abelard for the sake of those who read Latin and who might be interested in pursuing the parallels between the theses of the *Dialogue* and the positions Abelard himself takes in other works.

7. No English translation of the *Dialogue* has been done previously, but there is a French translation of the Migne text by M. De Gandillac which I sometimes found helpful, *Œuvres choisies d'Abélard* (Paris, 1945).

8. Abbreviations:

CC.CM 11   E. M. Buytaert, ed., *Petri Abaelardi opera theolo-*

gica ι. *Commentaria in Epistolam Pauli ad Romanos. Apologia contra Bernardum,* Corpus Christianorum, Continuatio Mediaevalis 11 (Turnholt, 1969).

cc.cm 12 E. M. Buytaert, ed., *Petri Abaelardi opera theologica* ιι. *Theologia christiana. Theologia 'Scholarium' (Recensiones breviores). Capitula haeresum Petri Abaelardi.* Corpus Christianorum, Continuatio Mediaevalis 12 (Turnholt, 1969).

pl. J. P. Migne, *Patrologiae cursus completus,* series latina.

9. Angle brackets < > indicate titles added by the translator; square brackets [ ] in the text indicate additions made by the translator for the sake of clarity and to avoid ambiguity.

A Dialogue of
a Philosopher with
a Jew, and a Christian

<Preface>[1]

I was looking about in a dream and suddenly three men, coming by different paths, stood before me.[2] While still dreaming, I asked them at once what their profession might be and why they had come to me.

They said: "We are men belonging to different religious schools of thought. Of course we all equally profess ourselves to be worshipers of the one God; however, we each serve him with a different faith and a different way of life. In fact, one of us who is a pagan from those they call philosophers, is content with the natural law. The other two possess sacred writings: one is called a Jew, the other a Christian. Now, for some time we have been discussing and arguing among ourselves about our different religious schools of thought, and we have finally agreed to submit to your judgment."

Greatly surprised at this, I asked who had led them or brought them together in this matter and particularly why they chose me as judge.

In reply the Philosopher said: "This was begun through my efforts since it is the proper task of philosophers to search into

---

[1] Manuscript inscriptions: "The Dialogue of Peter Baiolard," in Vienna, Österreichische Nationalbibliothek MS 819, fol. 1r; and "The Preface to the conferences of Peter Abaelard begins," in Oxford, Balliol College MS 296, fol. 161r.

[2] The first Latin word of the *Dialogue*, "aspiciebam," is used several times to introduce a vision in Dn 7.

the truth by rational means and in all things to follow not the opinion of men but the lead of reason. Therefore, after eagerly attending our schools for some time and being instructed in their rational methods as well as in their authorities, I was finally led to moral philosophy which is the goal of all disciplines, and I judged all other studies to be a foretaste of it. Immediately after learning as much as I could here about the supreme good and the supreme evil and about what makes a man blessed or miserable, I carefully examined the different religious schools of thought around me into which the world is now divided.[3] After I had examined all of them and compared

---

[3] In his poem to his son Astrolabe Abelard notes that the world is divided into so many religious schools of thought and contrary beliefs that each person follows the faith of his own tradition and does not submit the situation to rational investigation. I give the Latin text since it is not easily accessible:

Tot fidei sectis divisus mundus habetur
Ut quae sit vitae semita vix pateat.
Quod tot habet fidei contraria dogmata mundus
Quisquis facit generis traditione sui.
Denique nullus in his rationem consulere audet,
Dum quacumque sibi vivere pace studet.

"Le poème adressé par Abélard à son fils Astralabe," ed. B. Hauréau, *Notices et extraits des manuscrits de la Bibliothèque nationale et autres bibliothèques* 34.2 (1895) 167. (Throughout the *Dialogue* I translate *secta* and *secta fidei* as "school of thought" and "religious school of thought" respectively.) A similar point is made in *The Kuzari*: "There must no doubt be a way of acting, pleasing by its very nature, but not through the medium of intentions. If this be not so, why, then, do Christian and Moslim, who divide the inhabited world between them, fight with one another, each of them serving his God with pure intention, living either as monks or hermits, fasting and praying? For all that they vie with each other in committing murders, believing that this is a most pious work and brings them nearer to God. They fight in the belief that paradise and eternal bliss will be their reward. It is, however, impossible to agree with both." Judah Halevi, *The Kuzari*, p. 39 (part of the Philosopher's speech in this work).

them to one another, I resolved to follow the one most in harmony with reason.[4]

"So I turned my attention to the teaching of the Jews and the Christians and to the discussion of the faith and laws or reasons of both. I discovered the Jews to be stupid and the Christians insane, if I may say the latter without disturbing you who are called a Christian. I conferred with both for some time and since our dispute had not reached a conclusion we decided to submit the reasons for our respective cases to your judgment.

"We certainly knew that you are not ignorant of the power of philosophical reasons or of the defense raised by both Laws. For the Christian profession is so grounded in its own Law which they call the 'New Testament' that it does not presume to reject the Old; and it expends a great deal of zeal in the study of both. We had to choose some judge so that our dispute might reach an end, and we were only able to find someone who belonged to one of the three schools of thought."

And then as if expending the oil of flattery and anointing my head with this ointment, he immediately continued: "It is certain that the more you excel in intellectual acumen, and your broad learning is renowned, you are all the more suited to support or defend this judgment and able to satisfy the opposition of each of us. Indeed, that admirable work entitled *Theology*[5] which envy neither could bear with nor has

---

[4] This seems to be an echo of Cicero's definition of virtue: "For virtue is a habit of mind in harmony with reason and the order of nature." *De inventione* 2.53.159, tr. H. M. Hubbell, The Loeb Classical Library (Cambridge, Mass., 1949).

[5] Buytaert claims that a reference by Abelard to his *Theology* "means both his *Theologia 'Summa boni'* and *Theologia 'Scholarium'*. Consequently, if Abelard in another work refers to his *Theologia*, we must show good

prevailed to bear away, but which grows more gloriously under persecution,[6] is a sure proof to us of your intellectual acumen and in how much philosophical and sacred learning the treasury of your memory abounds, over and above the usual studies in your schools. From this it is evident that you have surpassed in both fields of learning not only you own masters but also others who have written in the whole range of learning."

Then I said: "I do not solicit the favor of this honor which you have reserved for me, since in the absence of wise men you have chosen a fool for a judge. For, accustomed as I am, like you, to the vain disputations of this world, I would not undertake a serious hearing on things with which I have been accustomed to be entertained. Yet you, O Philosopher, who profess no law and submit to reasons alone, do not over-estimate the advantage you may seem to have in this contest. Of course, there are two swords at your disposal for the fight, while the others are armed with only one against you. You can bring against them both reason and the written word, but they cannot use anything in the Law against you since you do not follow the Law; and indeed their use of reason is much less

---

reason before we identify it with one of the two." E. Buytaert, *Petri Abaelardi opera theologica* I. *Commentaria in Epistolam Pauli ad Romanos. Apologia contra Bernardum.* Corpus Christianorum. Continuatio Mediaevalis 11 (Turnholt, 1969), xxii. I have interpreted the expression "that admirable work" as a reference to a written product rather than as a general reference to theological activity.

    [6] Abelard uses similar language to describe the result of the treatment he received from the theologian, Anselm of Laon: "And the more open it was, the more it redounded to my credit, and by his persecution, he made me more esteemed." Tr. J. T. Muckle. *The Story of Abelard's Adversities.* A translation with notes of the *Historia calamitatum* (Toronto, 1954), p. 23.

powerful against you, to the extent that you, more practised in reasoning, have more abundant philosophical armor.

"Nonetheless, since you have set this up by agreement and mutual consent and I see that each of you has confidence in his own powers, our embarrassment should not interfere with your daring, particularly since I believe I will learn something from this. In fact, as one of your own reminds us: 'There is no teaching so false that there is not some true teaching mixed in.'[7] And I believe that there is no disputation so frivolous that it does not contain some instructive lesson. That is why that greatest of wise men, to get the attention of the reader, says at the very beginning of his Proverbs: 'A wise man by hearing will be wiser, an intelligent man will gain sound guidance.'[8] And James the Apostle says: 'Let every man be quick to hear but slow to speak.'"[9]

They gratefully approve of our agreement.[10]

---

[7] Augustine, *Libri duo quaestionum evangeliorum* 2.40 (PL 35: 1354).

[8] Prv 1, 5.

[9] Jas 1, 19.

[10] "The Preface ends. The first conference of the Philospher, namely with the Jew, begins." Added in Oxford, Balliol College MS 296, fol. 161v.

<The Philosopher and the Jew>

The Philosopher says: It is up to me, who am content with the natural law which is the first law, to be the first to question the others. I brought you together to inquire about the Scriptures which were subsequently added. I say "first," not only in time but also by nature. Surely, everything which is more simple is naturally prior to what is more multiple. But the natural law, that is, the knowledge of morals which we call ethics, consists solely of moral lessons. However, the teaching of your Laws adds to these certain precepts associated with external signs which seem to us to be completely superfluous; but we must consider these in their proper place.

They both grant to the Philosopher first place in the joining of the fight.

Then the Philosopher says: First, I ask you both together one thing which I see applies equally to both of you who are supported principally on Scripture: did some rational consideration induce you into your respective religious schools of thought, or do you here simply follow the opinion of men and the love of your own people? Indeed, the first of these, if it is true, must be highly approved, just as the latter must be totally rejected. However, I believe the conscience of no reasonable man will deny that the latter is true, particularly since we also see it borne out in numerous examples. For it often happens that when the husband or wife in a marriage is converted to a different religious school of thought, their children hold the firm faith of the parent with whom they remain. Upbringing is stronger in them than the origin of blood or reason since no matter by whom they are brought up, children will recognize those who brought them up as their fathers both in the faith and in their general upbringing. This fact was not hidden from him who said, "The Son cannot do anything but only what he sees the Father doing."[11] For there is such natural love in each and every man for his own people and for those with whom he is brought up that whatever is said against their faith is abhorrent to him. "Turning custom into nature,"[12] whatever children have learned they hold to obstinately as adults, and before they are able to understand what is said they claim to believe it; for as the poet reminds us, "A jar will retain the scent of what is first poured in it when new a very long time."[13] Indeed, some philosopher argues in this way when he says: be careful that you hold as sacred what you have received in youthful studies, since it often happens that an adult treatise of philosophy rejects things accommodated to youthful ears.[14]

For it is surprising that although human understanding grows throughout the ages and the succession of time in every-

[11] Jn 5, 19.

[12] Sallust, *War with Jugurtha* 85.9, tr. J. C. Rolfe, The Loeb Classical Library (Cambridge, Mass., rev. ed. 1931).

[13] Horace, *Epistolae* 1.2.69, tr. S. P. Bovie, *The Satires and Epistles of Horace* (Chicago, 1959).

[14] I have been unable to identify this philosopher. A similar expression is used later by Alan of Lille in which the words, "philosophiae senior tractatus eliminat" are identical in both Abelard and Alan, see Alan of Lille, *De planctu naturae* (PL 210: 451c), tr. D. M. Moffat, *The Complaint of Nature* by Alain de Lille, Yale Studies in English, 36 (New York, 1908), p. 39, line 199.

thing else, in the faith, in which error threatens the greatest peril, there is no advance. But youths as well as adults, the unlettered as well as the lettered, are said to feel the same way about the faith, and the one who does not go beyond the common understanding of the people is said to be most steadfast in the faith.[15] Surely the result of this is that no one is allowed to inquire into what should be believed among his own people or to doubt what everyone affirms, without fear of punishment. For it is embarrassing for men to be questioned about that to which they are incapable of responding. Surely, no one who doubts his own strength enters freely into a conflict, and it is the one who hopes for the victory who runs to battle of his own accord.[16] These even frequently burst into such insanity that they are not ashamed to declare that they believe what they admit they are unable to understand, as if faith consists in the utterance of words rather than in the understanding of the mind, and as if faith were more a matter of the mouth than of the heart. Hence, they take the greatest glory in their apparent belief in what can be neither expressed in words nor conceived by the mind.[17] The attachment of each

[15] See Heloise: "I am judged religious at a time when there is little in religion which is not hypocrisy, when whoever does not offend the opinions of men receives the highest praise." Letter 3, tr. B. Radice, *The Letters of Abelard and Heloise* (Penguin Books, 1974), pp. 133-134.

[16] See Jerome: "I do not wish to fight in hope of victory, lest the day come when I lose the battle." *Contra Vigilantium* 16 (PL 23: 367B). The text is quoted in Letter 3, Heloise to Abelard, tr. B. Radice, p. 136.

[17] Abelard writes of his students: "They had kept asking of me rational and philosophical expositions and insisting on what could be understood and not mere declarations, saying that a flow of words is useless if reason does not follow them, that nothing is believed unless it first be understood and that it is ridiculous for a man to proclaim to others what neither he nor his

to his own school of thought even makes them so presumptuous and proud that whomever they see separated in faith from themselves, they judge to be estranged from the mercy of God, and with everyone else condemned, they will declare that they alone will be blessed.

And so, after contemplating this blindness and pride of the human race for some time, I turned to the divine mercy, begging it without end to deign to lead me out of such a great chasm of errors and such a miserable Charybdis, and to direct me out of such great storms to the port of salvation.[18] Now you see me eager for this, like a student enthusiastically intent on the instruction of your responses.

JEW: Indeed, you question two together, but two cannot conveniently respond together lest a multitude of speakers get in the way of understanding. If it is agreeable, I shall respond first because we were the first to come to the worship of God, or we received the first discipline[19] of the Law. Indeed, that brother there who professes himself to be a Christian, where

pupils can grasp by their intelligence." Tr. J. T. Muckle, *The Story of Abelard's Adversities*, p. 39.

[18] The mention of the port of salvation is reminiscent of the Preface to Augustine's *The Happy Life*, tr. L. Schopp, in The Fathers of the Church, 1 (New York, 1948), pp. 43-50.

[19] "Discipline" translates the Latin word *disciplina* which frequently connotes a training leading to desired behavior, in addition to connoting an intellectual branch of knowledge. In this and similar contexts both connotations seem to be present. Abelard's use of the term in this first dialogue does not reflect the speculative sense of the term as much as the pedagogical sense. For the medieval use of the term see M. D. Chenu, "Notes de lexicographie philosophique médiévale: 'Disciplina,'" *Revue des sciences philosophiques et théologiques* 25 (1936) 686-692.

he sees me deficient or less able, will supply what is wanting in my imperfection. Armed as it were with two horns, grasping as he does the two Testaments, he will be all the stronger to resist and to fight the enemy.

PHILOSOPHER: I agree.

JEW: However, I wish to caution you about this one thing before the contest of our proposed conference. If you should perhaps seem to overpower my simplicity by the strength of philosophical reasons, you should not boast that you have been victorious over us on that account. Nor should you turn the foolishness of one little man into the disgrace of a whole people, nor convict the faith because of one man's deficiency, nor falsely accuse the faith of error because I fail somewhat in discussing it.

PHILOSOPHER: And this also seems to be prudently said, but it was prefaced unnecessarily since you should not doubt that I will work to seek out the truth, not to show off; I will not wrangle like a sophist, but will examine reasons like a philosopher; and what is of most importance, I am seeking the salvation of my soul.

JEW: May the Lord himself, who seems to have inspired you with this zeal to inquire with so much care for the salvation of your soul, grant us that through this conference you may be able to find him to your advantage. Now it remains for me to respond to the questions as far as he grants.

PHILOSOPHER: Certainly, this accords with the terms of our proposal.

JEW: Indeed, it is clear that while they are children and do not yet enjoy the age of discretion, people follow the faith and custom of those men with whom they live and especially of those whom they love more dearly. But after they are adults and so can then be guided by their own choice, they ought to be committed to their own judgment and not to that of another; and it is not as proper to follow opinion as to investigate the truth. I have mentioned these things beforehand because affection of kin and the custom which we first learned perhaps did lead us initially to our faith, but now reason rather than opinion keeps us here.

PHILOSOPHER: I beg of you to reveal this reason to us and it will be enough.

JEW: If that Law which we follow was given by God, as we believe, then we should not be censured for obeying it; on the contrary, we should be rewarded for obedience, and those who hold it in contempt are in grave error. Now even if we cannot convince you that it was given by God, you, on the other hand, are unable to refute this position. However, let us take an example from the practice of human life, and I ask you to advise me in the matter.

Suppose I am a slave of some master whom I am extremely afraid of offending, and I have many fellow slaves who are inspired with the same fear. They tell me that our master gave all his slaves an order in my absence, but I am ignorant of it. They are carrying it out and they exhort me to do the same.

What do you advise me to do if I should have a doubt about an order given in my absence? I do not believe that you or anyone else are going to advise me to despise the counsel of all the slaves and, following my own opinion, dissociate myself from what they are all carrying out, and which they all testify was the master's order. This is so, particularly since the command seems to be such that it cannot be refuted on rational grounds. Why must I be in doubt about a danger when I can be safe from it?[20] If the master ordered what is confirmed by the testimony of many and which seems quite reasonable, it is completely inexcusable for me not to obey. If, however, deceived by the advice or encouragement and example of my fellow slaves, I do what was not commanded, even if it was not to be done, it must be charged against them rather than against me, since it was respect for the master which drew me to perform the action.

PHILOSOPHER: Certainly, you yourself have provided the advice which you requested, and no sensible person would disagree. But apply the example of this proposed analogy to what we are striving for.

JEW: As you yourself know, for many past generations our people have obediently observed this Testament which they affirm was given to them by God, and they likewise instructed all those who came after them in its observance, both by word and by example. Almost the whole world agrees that this Law

---

[20] See Jerome: "What need is there to foresake what is certain and pursue uncertainty? *Contra Vigilantium* 16 (PL. 23: 367B). The text is quoted in Letter 3, Heloise to Abelard, tr. B. Radice, p. 136.

was given to us by God. If we are perhaps unable to convince unbelievers of this, there is no one, however, who can provide a rational refutation of what we believe.

It is surely an act of piety and completely in harmony with reason, and fitting as well to the divine goodness and to human salvation, to believe that God takes such great care of men that he also deigned to instruct them by a written Law and to restrain our malice at least through fear of punishments. For if the laws of secular princes were instituted beneficially for this purpose, who would deny that the highest and most beneficent Prince would also have had such concern? For how will one be able to govern a subject people without a law if, for instance, each, abandoned to his own will, should follow his own choice? Or how will one repress their malice by justly punishing evildoers unless a law were established beforehand which forbade the evils from being done? For this reason, I believe it is clear that divine Law came to men in the past that the world also might receive from God the beginning and authority of this boon, when he wished to restrain malice through the institution of laws. Otherwise, it could easily have appeared that God had no concern for human affairs, and that the state of the world is run by chance rather than ruled by providence.

If, indeed, one believes that a Law was given to the world by God, which has greater claim to being this Law than ours which has received such great authority from its antiquity and the common opinion of men? Suppose, finally, that I am in doubt, just like you, whether God instituted this Law which, however, is confirmed by so many witnesses and by reason. You are bound, nonetheless, according to the conclusion of the above analogy, to advise me to obey it, particularly since my own conscience bids me to it.

I, along with you, have a common faith in the truth of the one God; I perhaps love him as much as you, and besides, I exhibit this love through works which you do not have. If these works are not useful, what harm do they do me even if they were not commanded, since they were not forbidden? And who could censure me if I work more generously for the Lord, even when I am not bound by any precept? Who would censure this faith which, as was said, greatly commends the divine goodness and enkindles in us a great charity towards him who is so solicitous for our salvation that he deigns to instruct us by a written Law? Therefore, either make a specific accusation against this Law or stop inquiring why we follow it.

Whoever thinks that our persevering zeal, which puts up with so much, is without reward, affirms that God is most cruel. Surely, no people is known or is even believed to have endured so much for God as we constantly put up with for him; and no one ought to claim that there can be any dross of sin which the furnace of this affliction has not burned away. Dispersed among all the nations, alone, without an earthly king or prince, are we not burdened with such great demands that almost every day of our miserable lives we pay the debt of an intolerable ransom? In fact, we are judged deserving of such great contempt and hatred by all that anyone who inflicts some injury on us believes it to be the greatest justice and the highest sacrifice offered to God. For they believe that the misfortune of such a great captivity has only befallen us because of God's supreme wrath, and they count as just vengeance whatever cruelty they visit on us, whether they be Christians or pagans. The pagans, indeed, remembering the oppressions of long ago by which we first occupied their territory and afterwards weakened and destroyed them through continual persecutions, reckon as just vengeance whatever they inflict on us. The Christians, however, seem to have a greater cause for persecuting us because, as they say, we killed their Lord.

Consider the kind of people among whom we wander in exile and in whose patronage we must have confidence! We entrust our lives to our greatest enemies and are compelled to believe in the faith of those without faith. Sleep itself, which brings the greatest rest and renews nature, disquiets us with such great worry that even while sleeping we can think of nothing but the danger that looms over our throats. No pathway except the path to heaven appears safe for us whose very dwelling place is dangerous. When we go to neighboring places we hire a guard at no small price, in whom we have little confidence. The princes themselves who rule over us and for whose patronage we pay dearly desire our death all the more to such a degree that they then snatch away the more freely what we possess. Confined and constricted in this way as if the whole world had conspired against us alone, it is a wonder that we are allowed to live. We are allowed to possess neither fields nor vineyards nor any landed estates because there is no one who can protect them for us from open or occult attack. Consequently, the principal gain that is left for us is that we sustain our miserable lives here by lending money at interest to strangers; but this just makes us most hateful to them who think they are being oppressed by it. However, more than any tongue can do, our very situation is enough to speak more eloquently to all of the supreme misery of our lives and of the dangers in which we ceaselessly labor.[21]

---

[21] For a discussion of Jewish life in Medieval Europe about this time see

The amount of difficulty which the precepts of the Law
involve is not unknown to anyone who considers it, so that we
are afflicted as intolerably by the yoke of the Law as by the
oppression of men. Who would not abhor or fear to receive the
very sacrament of our circumcision, whether out of shame or
because of the pain? What part of the human body is as tender
as the one on which the Law inflicts that wound, and it does so
on small infants too? What is as bitter as the wild herbs which
we eat in the seasoning of the paschal sacrifice?[22] Who does
not also see that almost all delicious foods, particularly those
that can be easily obtained, are forbidden us? Whatever meats
beasts have already tasted are unclean for us, and animals
which have died of suffocation or natural causes are forbidden
us.[23] We are only allowed to eat those animals which we
ourselves have slaughtered and whose fat and veins we have
carefully removed.[24] This is no small burden for us,
particularly since we do not have sufficient means to buy the
whole beef. For just as we abhor flesh slaughtered by Gentiles,
so they abhor flesh prepared by us, and we all likewise abstain
from wine prepared by strangers.

From this it is clear how much difficulty our exiled sojourn
among you endures for God. Who, finally, would not abhor

S. W. Baron, *A Social and Religious History of the Jews*, Vol. IV. *Meeting of East and West*, 2nd rev. ed. (New York, 1957).

[22] See Ex 12, 8.

[23] See Ex 22, 30; Lv 17, 15; Ez 4, 14.

[24] This is a curious statement. While there was a Biblical command to remove the blood from meat (Lv 3, 17; 7, 26; 17, 10-14; and Dt 12, 16.23), there is no such command to remove the veins from slaughtered animals which were to be eaten. I assume "veins" here is a general reference to blood.

not only undertaking the austerity of our legal penalties but even inflicting them on criminals? Who would put up with taking a tooth for a tooth, an eye for an eye, and even a soul for a soul from his brother?[25] To say nothing of the one who consents to take these things on himself lest he be in conflict with the Law. Surely, from these observances and innumerable others it is clear that each of us who obeys the Law truthfully confesses to God with the Psalmist: "According to the words of your lips, I have kept hard ways."[26]

PHILOSOPHER: In truth, this zeal which you seem to have for God puts up with many and great things, whatever the intent may be; but what is more important is whether this intent is correct or erroneous. There is certainly no school of religious thought which does not believe itself to be a friend of God and which does not perform those actions for his sake which it thinks please him. But you do not on this account approve of the school of thought of everyone, but strive to defend yours alone or to place it far ahead of the others. Nonetheless, I want you to consider to what an extent this position is incompatible with reason, and I will prove it from the written Law itself which you follow.[27]

JEW: And this I freely accept.

[25] See Ex 21. 24.
[26] Ps 17. 4.
[27] In the following discussion with the Jew the Philosopher insists on certain themes which reflect positions of Abelard. These are: (1) the Patriarchs before the Law were justified by the natural law without the Jewish Law; (2) circumcision did not confer justification; (3) the legal observances of the Law did not confer justification; (4) the Law does not promise spiritual reward after death.

PHILOSOPHER: It is certain that before the handing on of the Law or the observance of legal sacraments most people were content with the natural law which consists in the love of God and neighbor; they fostered justice and were most acceptable to God.[28] This was the case, for example, with Abel, Enoch, Noah and his sons, and Abraham too, and Lot, and Melchizedek whom your own Law even commemorates and highly commends. Indeed, of those, Enoch is mentioned as being so pleasing to God that the Lord is said to have taken him alive into paradise, as one of your own affirms in these words: "Enoch pleased God and was taken up into paradise that he may give an example of repentance to the nations."[29] And of Noah it is written, "a good man and blameless in that age."[30] The Lord left a clear example of how much he loved him when he saved only Noah and his household to be the seed of the human race after all others were drowned in the flood.

And add to these your outstanding patriarchs Abraham, Isaac, and Jacob in whom and in whose seed the future

---

[28] See in particular Abelard, Sermon 3 (PL 178: 398B-399A). Here Abelard claims that the natural law more truly justified the pagans than the written law the Jews. Notice that the Philosopher claims that the natural law consists in the love of God and neighbor. On this point the natural law, in Abelard's view, resembles the Christian Law and differs from the Jewish Law, as we shall see below. See Abelard, *Commentaria in Epistolam Pauli ad Romanos* 1, in *Petri Abaelardi opera theologica* I. *Commentaria in Epistolam Pauli ad Romanos. Apologia contra Bernardum*, ed. by Eligius Buytaert, Corpus Christianorum. Continuatio Mediaevalis 11 (Turnholt, 1969), 84, and "For if we carefully consider the moral precepts of the Gospel we will find nothing more than a reformation of natural law which the philosophers clearly followed" (Abelard, *Theol. christ.*, 2.44, CC.CM 12: 149).

[29] Sir 44, 16.

[30] Gn 6, 9.

blessing of all peoples is promised. These even came before the Law, but consider how their privileges were more excellent than those of others who lived after the Law. Whence, God is said to be particularly theirs, and when the Lord was angry with the people, Moses himself, the lawgiver, placated him by recalling the merits of the patriarchs and the promises made to them. For it is written:

> But Moses implored the Lord, saying: Let your blazing wrath die down and be appeased upon the wickedness of your people. Remember your servants, Abraham, Isaac, and Israel, to whom you swore by your own self, saying: I will make your descendants as numerous as the stars in the sky; and all this land that I have spoken of I will give your descendants; and you shall possess it forever. So the Lord relented in the punishment he had threatened to inflict on his people.[31]

It is clearly gathered from this how acceptable to God was that spontaneous obedience of the earlier fathers, an obedience to which no law constrained them up to that time and a liberty in which we still serve him.

But if you claim that in some way the Law had begun in Abraham because of the sacrament of circumcision, you will surely find that he receives no reward from God for it, lest it be a cause for boasting on your part because of the Law; and he did not receive any justification nor is he commended by the Lord for it. In fact, it is written that he, like the earlier fathers, was justified by faith when not yet circumcised, when it is said, "Abraham put his faith in God and it was credited to him as an act of justice."[32] Abraham's religion too dated from before he

---

[31] Ex 32, 11-14.
[32] Gn 15, 6; see Abelard, *Comm. Rom.* 2, cc.cm 11: 143-144.

had received the promise of the land or the promise of the future multiplication, whether for himself or for his seed. Even after he was circumcised and when he heard from the Lord that all peoples were to be blessed in him or in his seed, he did not merit this because of circumcision but because of the obedience whereby he was willing to sacrifice his son.[33] Finally, if you consider the whole history of your Testament you will find no reward promised for circumcision, but only that the Lord established that whoever of the seed of Abraham was not circumcised, that person would not be counted among his people, that is, among the sons of Abraham. In fact, it is written that the Lord said as much to Abraham:

> I will establish my covenant between you and me and your descendants after you, etc. This is the covenant which you will keep. Every male among you shall be circumcised. An infant of eight days old shall be circumcised among you. If a male is uncircumcised, that is, if the flesh of his foreskin has not been cut away, that soul will perish out of his people, etc.[34]

And if you should say that this perishing must also be understood in reference to the damnation of the soul, then a measure of the irrationality of the institution of circumcision is the greater danger of not having it, since there was no danger of this kind in the past when it did not exist. This interpretation even bars the kingdom of heaven to infants who die before the eighth day but who had not yet done any evil to merit damnation.

Pay careful attention to the reward which the Lord promises and fixes for the observance of the whole Law. You can surely

---

[33] See Gn 22, 17-18.
[34] Gn 17, 7.10.12.14.

expect nothing from him for this except earthly prosperity, since you see nothing else promised there.[35] And since it is not clear whether you would even receive this, you who on your own admission are afflicted more than all mortals, it is not a little surprising this hope which you place in obedience to the Law and on account of which you put up with so much and so many things, since surely you were frustrated precisely in the benefit which you must have particularly expected because of the obligation arising from the promise. Consequently, either you are not fulfilling the Law and so you incur the legal curse of damnation, or the one who made the promise to those who fulfill the Law is not true to his promises. But whatever of these you choose, I see that you must not place your trust in the Law. A reward consisting only of earthly things would so little measure up to beatitude that the life you could expect would be no different for you than for beasts of burden.

If you are confident that observance is so worthwhile for you that it merits the beatitude of eternal life as well as prosperity in this life, why, I ask, when God was inviting you to the observance of the Law by proposing a reward, did he promise the minimum reward but keep utterly silent about the maximum ? He surely did not speak with any discernment if he knew that both were granted for obedience to the Law when, that is, he completely passed over the one which could have been most persuasive. As was said, no mention was made in the reward of that true and eternal beatitude, but earthly

[35] See Abelard. *Comm. Rom.* 2. CC.CM 11: 190, 191, and "We know that the Jews received no heavenly promise as a remuneration for their obedience, but only an abundance of earthly things is established as a reward for them." Sermon 5 (PL 178: 424A).

prosperity is proposed to such an extent that it alone is established as the motive for obedience, and it is commended so far as to be considered to count as a satisfactory response to every inquiry made by posterity. Accordingly, it is written that Moses the lawgiver, while instructing the people against any disobedience against the Law, says:

> Hear, O Israel! Keep the commandments of the Lord, your God, and the ordinances and statutes he has enjoined on you. And do what is right and good in the sight of the Lord, that you may, according to his word, prosper, and enter in and possess the good land which the Lord promised on oath to your fathers, thrusting all your enemies out of your way. Later on, when your son asks you what these ordinances and statutes and decrees mean which the Lord, our God, has enjoined on us, you shall say to him: We were once slaves of Pharaoh in Egypt, but the Lord brought us out of Egypt with his strong hand and wrought before our eyes signs and wonders, great and dire, in Egypt against Pharaoh and his whole house. And he brought us from there to lead us into the land he promised on oath to our fathers, and to give it to us. And the Lord commanded us to observe all these statutes in fear of the Lord, our God, that we may always have as prosperous and happy a life as we have today.[36]

Again:

> The Lord your God has chosen you from all the nations on the face of the earth to be a people peculiarly his own. Observe, therefore, the commandments and statutes and decrees which I enjoin on you today. If you observe them and carry them out, the Lord your God will also keep his covenant with you and the mercy which he promised on oath to your fathers. And he will

[36] Dt 6, 4.17-24.

love you and multiply you and he will bless the fruit of your womb and the produce of your soil, the grain and wine and corn and oil, and the herds, and the flocks of your sheep, in the land which he swore to your fathers he would give you. You will be blessed above all peoples; no man or woman among you shall be childless nor shall your livestock be barren. He will remove all sickness from you; and he will not afflict you with any of the malignant diseases that you know from Egypt, but will afflict all your enemies. You shall consume all the nations which the Lord, your God, will deliver up to you.[37]

And again:

He will give to your land the early rain and the late rain, that you may gather in your grain, wine, and oil, and the hay out of the fields to feed your cattle and that you may eat your fill.[38]

And all these blessings will come upon you and overwhelm you, if you hearken to his precepts. May you be blessed in the city, and blessed in the country. Blessed be the fruit of your womb, and the produce of your soil and the offspring of your livestock, the issue of your herds, and the folds of your sheep. Blessed be your grain bins and blessed your stores. May you be blessed in your coming in and going out. And he will bless all your undertakings. And you will lend to many nations and borrow from none.[39]

So you see that in recompense for keeping the Law a blessing is promised to men such as is found in the fruit of your beasts of burden and in your herds of cattle and in your sheep folds. But no mention is made of the spiritual blessing of the

[37] Dt 7, 6.11-16.
[38] Dt 11, 14-15.
[39] Dt 28, 2-6.12.

soul. Nor is anything promised to those who are obedient, or to transgressors, in what concerns the salvation or damnation of the soul; but only earthly benefits or disadvantages are mentioned and the greatest benefits are passed over entirely.

So I ask whether how, after the Law has been given to you, the natural law can still be sufficient for salvation for some people without, that is, those external works peculiar to the Law, even as it was in times past? You cannot reasonably deny this since it is certain that this Law was given only to you, not to other peoples, and circumcision was enjoined only on Abraham and on his seed. Indeed, only those born of Isaac belong to his seed, as the Lord says to Abraham, "For it is through Isaac that descendants shall bear your name."[40] And after he had instituted the covenant of circumcision he added, "But my covenant I will maintain with Isaac."[41]

The pagan Job who, you do not doubt, lived after Abraham and without the Law, the Lord commended so far as to say, "that there is none on earth like him, blameless and upright, fearing God and avoiding evil."[42] While demonstrating to us his own justice which we should imitate, Job makes no mention of the works of the Law, but only the works of the natural law of which natural reason itself convinces each and every one. When he says, "If I have walked in vanity and my foot has hastened to deceit; if I have denied to the poor what they desired and allowed the eyes of the widow to languish, etc.,"[43] he established by words and examples the law, as it were, for us people.

[40] Gn 21, 12.
[41] Gn 17, 21.
[42] Jb 1, 8.
[43] Jb 31, 5.16.

Whence Solomon asserts that the prayers of both pagans and Jews are to be heard when he says:

> Moreover the foreigner, likewise, who is not of your people Israel, when he comes from a distant land to honor you and prays in this place, then listen from your heavenly dwelling place. Do all that the foreigner asks of you, that all the peoples of the earth may learn to fear your name as do your people Israel.[44]

So you see, when it is promised that the prayers of strangers are to be heard and everything carried out, and you even make them fear God just as you do, who would still despair of their salvation, since it is written, "Happy the man who fears the Lord,"[45] and again, "For there is no want to them that fear God."[46]

Finally, Scripture recalls that your own Jeremiah, who existed long after the institution of circumcision and the sacraments of the Law and who certainly was of the seed of Abraham, was sanctified before he was born. The Lord said to him, "Before I formed you in the womb I knew you; and before you were born I sanctified you."[47] How, I ask, do you say those things are necessary for your salvation and sanctification, when he was sanctified without them before he was even born? Or what was his sanctification then unless, perhaps, through the inspiration of God he then already believed God and loved him? Surely, these two [faith and love] are in some people and undoubtedly made Jeremiah just, whatever was as yet externally wanting in him.

---

[44] 1 Kgs 8, 41-43.
[45] Ps 112, 1.
[46] See Ps 34, 10.
[47] Jer 1, 5.

If these were sufficient for the salvation of some people before the Law or even now, why was it necessary to add the yoke of the Law and to increase transgressions through the multiplication of precepts? For where there is no law, there can be no violation of the law. And anyone desires something so much the more eagerly, the more he feels that he is kept from it and restrained as if by some force. As the poet says, "We strive after what is forbidden and we desire what is denied."[48] One of your own, giving this careful thought and clearly showing that no one is justified by the works of the Law, says, "For the Law serves only to bring down wrath, for where there is no law there is no transgression."[49] Moreover, demonstrating that your Law not only does not take away sin but even truly increases it, he added a little further on, "Now the Law came in order to increase offenses."[50] And again he says:

> It was only through the law that I came to know sin. I should never have known what evil desire was unless the Law had said: Thou shalt not covet. Sin seized that opportunity; it used the commandment to rouse in me every kind of evil desire. For without the law sin was dead. At first I lived without law, but when the commandment came, sin came to life and I died. The commandment that should have led to life was discovered in my case to be unto death.[51]

---

[48] Ovid, *Amores* 3.4.17, tr. G. Showerman, The Loeb Classical Library (Cambridge, Mass., 1921).

[49] Rom 4, 15.

[50] Rom 5, 20.

[51] Rom 7, 7-10.

Indeed, though I know that you in no way acknowledge these testimonies, it is clear nonetheless that the conscience of no reasonable man disagrees with them.

How did he constitute you a people special to himself by giving the Law, and why does he call Israel his firstborn whom such a great burden weighs down for no reason? Who could even excuse you from the curse of the Law, you who, because of your sins, as you admit yourselves, have lost the promised land outside of which you can in no way fulfill the Law? Because of this you are not permitted to exercise the vengeance of your justice, nor are you allowed to celebrate the sacrifices or the offerings instituted to cleanse away sins, nor can you even carry out the canticles of the divine praises. You yourselves even acknowledge this, saying, "How shall we sing a song of the Lord in a foreign land?"[52] From this it is clear that the works as well as the words of the Law and likewise its reward have been lost. Nor can you nor your wives be cleansed now through the sacrifices and offerings which have been lost. You cannot be consecrated to the Lord since you are deprived alike of priesthood and temple, so that you do not have the solace of earthly dignity, you who asked only earthly things from the Lord and who have only received the promise of an earthly reward, as was said.

JEW: You have raised a whole series of objections which are difficult to keep track of with a view to replying to each of them in order. I shall try to reply to them as they occur to me.

Even if we conceded that men can still be saved now by the natural law alone in the manner of the holy men of old, that is,

[52] Ps 137, 4.

without circumcision or the other carnal prescriptions of the
written Law, it must not, however, be conceded that these
latter were superfluous additions on that account. They are
very useful in increasing or in more safely protecting religion
and in more successfully repressing evil. Let us take some of
the arguments you yourself have proposed.

As long as believers were scattered throughout the
population of unbelievers and the Lord had not yet given them
a land of their own, they were not divided by the observance of
a law from those with whom they had to live, lest the
dissimilarity of life styles should have given rise to enmity.
However, after the Lord led Abraham from his own land and
his own people to give to him and to his seed a land as an
inheritance through which they would be separated from the
Gentiles, he also decreed to separate them completely by means
of the corporeal works of the Law so that the more they were
separated from them both geographically and bodily, the less
chance there would be that the believers could be corrupted by
the unbelievers. Consequently, after the promise was made to
Abraham and to his seed of the land in which the Lord would
gather a people to himself and constitute them, as it were, his
own nation, straightway he correctly began to set up the Law
according to which they were to live there, beginning with
circumcision.[53] Of course, the Lord knew how stiff the necks of
our people would be and that they were easily inclined to the
idolatry and evil ways of the pagans, as was afterwards borne

---

[53] The same expression, "beginning with circumcision" is used by
Abelard in Sermon 3 (PL. 178: 402A). The image of the Law as a wall set up
between the chosen people and their neighbors is also used in this sermon;
the material of the Jew's discussion here is to be found at some length in
Sermon 3.

out in fact. So, when the legal observances were interposed like a wall, he decreed that their rituals would set them apart in such a way that they would be bound to the pagans by no society founded on mutual dealings or friendship, and indeed they would beget from this perpetual enmities directed against themselves.

It is customary, in fact, to have the greatest familiarity among people through the union of matrimony and the association of meals; so, to remove these two occasions completely, the Lord instituted circumcision and forbade us to eat delicious foods.

For the sign of circumcision seems so abhorrent to the Gentiles that if we were to seek their women, the women would in no way give their consent, believing that the truncating of this member is the height of foulness, and detesting the divine sign of holiness as an idolatry.[54] Or even if they were to offer us their consent in this, we would shrink in horror from associating that member with the foulness of unbelieving women – that member sanctified to the Lord precisely through that sign by which we enter into a convenant with him alone. And out of reverence for this sign, Abraham, binding his servant by an oath, compelled him to put his hand to his thigh so that the servant would so much more surely protect himself from perjury, the more attention he paid to the greater holiness of this member.[55]

---

[54] The usual word used to speak about circumcision is *signum* (= sign). The word used here is *signaculum* and while elsewhere (*Comm. Rom.* 2, CC.CM 11: 128-129) Abelard recognises a difference between the two terms in the context of the discussion of circumcision, this difference does not seem to be suggested here.

[55] See Gn 24, 2 and Abelard, *Comm. Rom.* 2, CC.CM 11: 131.

Accordingly, the Lord forbids us to marry pagans and above all those pagans whose land we were to possess, saying somewhere: "Take care you never join in friendship with the inhabitants of the land which may be your ruin. Neither shall you take their daughters as wives for your sons lest they make your sons commit fornication with their gods."[56] And Rebekah, foreseeing this long before, compelled her son Jacob, on command of Isaac his father, to go to Mesopotamia to take a wife from her people there. As it is written: "And Rebekah said to Isaac: I am disgusted with my life because of the daughters of Heth. If Jacob takes a wife of the stock of this land I choose not to live. Isaac therefore called Jacob, etc."[57]

Whence, even if other reasons are not adduced, I believe these are enough for now. However, I believe your effort to weaken or diminish the merit of circumcision or of the Law by the very authority of Scripture can be refuted by this authority if, for example, you were to pay careful attention to those texts of Scripture which you seem to have passed over in silence, and which I believe you saw would be harmful to your position. For when he instituted the covenant which was entered into with the Lord through circumcision, he said to Abraham: "I will establish my covenant between you and me and your descendants after you throughout the ages as an ever-lasting pact, to be your God and the God of your descendants after you."[58] For when he says "as a perpetual covenant, that I may be a God to you and to your descendants" he clearly teaches that we are to be covenanted to God forever by circum-

---

[56] Ex 34. 12.16.
[57] Gn 27. 46 - 28. 1.
[58] Gn 17. 7.

cision and for this reason we are deserving to have him as God, so that neither in this life nor in the future are we separated from him. He himself repeats this to reinforce our memory when he adds: "And my covenant shall be in your flesh as an everlasting pact."[59] That is to say, just as circumcision once accomplished in the flesh cannot now be undone, so neither can we be separated any more from God who, comforting us in a special way, says, "I will take you as my own people, and you shall have me as your God."[60]

Consequently, he calls himself in a special way the God of the Hebrews, not only the God of Abraham, Isaac, and Jacob. Indeed, it is suggested that he becomes the God of Abraham and of his sons to such a degree through circumcision that, before circumcision, he was not called the God of them or of men. However, he instituted circumcision as a fitting sign of the covenant between himself and us, so that those who are conceived through that member which is specially consecrated after obediently receiving circumcision, are also admonished to sanctify themselves to the Lord through the very instrument of their conception. In this way they are circumcised interiorly in the heart from vices, just as already they were outwardly circumcised in the flesh. And in this way they cut themselves off from their previous origin among the unbelieving Chaldeans through customs, just as they removed the front part of that member from themselves, departing from among them with Abraham not so much in body as in mind, as David recalls when he invites the faithful soul in these words: "Forget your people and your father's house, etc."[61]

[59] Gn 17, 13.
[60] See Ex 6, 7.
[61] Ps 45, 11.

This is why the Lord, comparing the people to a choice vineyard, complained that he had expected "it to yield grapes but it yielded wild grapes."[62] And just as the whole people is compared to a vineyard, so each male believer is properly compared to the vines and their genitals to the shoots of the vines. However, a shoot of a vine yields wild grapes rather than grapes and remains wild unless it is pruned. So, through this comparison the cutting away of the foreskin signifies the care of the divine husbandry towards us by which God made a beginning of our cultivation.

And if you would also reflect on the beginnings of human sin in the first parents and on the Lord's sentence of punishment issued against the woman when it is said to her, "In pain shall you bring forth children,"[63] you will also see the male participant in sin justly sharing punishment, particularly in the genital member. This is so that he might justly suffer precisely in that member by which he brings into the exile of the present life children who will die, casting himself and us from paradise into the trials of this life by his own sin. For it is right that woman, who suffers in childbirth, suffer from that member by which she conceives and gives birth, and that she be punished in childbirth for the very pleasure of concupiscence which she enjoyed in conception. And besides, she paid the penalty which she deserved by sinning. Because she sinned first and afterwards drew the man to sin, it was not unfitting that she should also go before him in punishment itself. But God did not entirely put off punishing the man who was immediately placed under a penalty, as the Lord said: "Cursed

[62] Is 5, 2.
[63] Gn 3, 16.

be the ground in your work. In toil shall you eat its yield all the days of your life. Thorns and thistles shall it bring forth to you, etc."[64]

But where we obtained the richness of the promised land which does not produce thorns and thistles, since the punishment is lessened there, circumcision not incongruously makes up for it. Yet after the promise of this land, before it was obtained, circumcision was immediately initiated by the patriarchs to convey a stronger authority to those coming after. I think this is enough for now on the reason for circumcision.

You, in your attempt to claim on the basis of Scripture that circumcision is only enjoined on those who are of Abraham's seed, do not notice that the same is also written of those who were not of his stock. For when the Lord first said, "Throughout the ages, every male among you, when he is eight days old, shall be circumcised, including the houseborn slave and the slave acquired with money shall be circumcised," he immediately added, "and whoever is not of your blood."[65] Consider how much discrepancy there is in your claim that circumcision applies to Isaac alone and to his seed, and correct yourself on the basis of what Abraham did. On the Lord's command he is said to have circumcised Ishmael along with himself and all the men in his house, the slaves born in the house as well as those who were bought and also aliens. Scripture says, "immediately, on the very day that the Lord commanded him" before Isaac was yet born, so that you would know that it began with your ancestors and that you

[64] Gn 3, 17-18.
[65] Gn 17, 12.

would more readily adopt it as your own as being more natural.

Now if it is agreeable, let us also present the very words of Scripture which are in this vein: "Then Abraham took his son Ishmael and all his household slaves and he circumcised the flesh of their foreskins on that same day, as the Lord had told him to do."[66] And again: "On that same day Abraham and his son Ishmael were circumcised; and all the male members of his household, including the slaves born in his house or acquired with his money and foreigners, were circumcised with him."[67]

There is nothing to stop you from claiming that the expression "I will make my covenant with Isaac"[68] refers only to the covenant of circumcision and not to the promised land, as long as you grant what has already been said: "I will establish my covenant with him as an everlating pact and with his descendants after him."[69] For even if Ishmael was also circumcised on command of the Lord, nevertheless, the Lord did not establish circumcision in him in whose posterity it has not remained.

There are no grounds for your adducing the pagan Job as an example, since you cannot prove he was uncircumcised or that he lived after the institution of circumcision. For it is clear that just as Ishmael was circumcised by Abraham, so were Esau and Jacob, and both the outcast sons as well as the chosen were circumcised by the patriarchs according to the command of the Lord, so that from then on their descendants, if they should

---

[66] Gn 17, 23.
[67] Gn 17, 26-27.
[68] Gn 17, 21.
[69] Gn 17, 19.

adhere to God, would receive the example of circumcision. Accordingly, you yourselves even today keep the practice in imitation of Ishmael your father when you receive circumcision at the age of twelve.[70] We know that our people had many proselytes from the Gentiles who were converted to the Law, and this surely not so much out of imitation of their parents as out of a kindred virtue. This could also have been the case with Job who, we see, even offered sacrifices acceptable to God according to our practice for his sons as well as for his friends.

As to the objection that only temporal and earthly reward was promised for the observance of the whole Law, and that the Lord did not speak wisely in his persuasion or recommendation concerning the Law if the fulfillment of the legal precepts was not also to merit eternal life, this can easily be refuted, since, as I said, it is also by circumcision which the Law commanded that we were covenanted with the Lord forever. Besides, why did he choose us from among the nations

[70] While this is not conclusive evidence that the Philosopher himself was circumcised, it is clearly a reference to his social and cultural origins. This reference has suggested to some that Abelard's Philosopher is himself an Arab, one of the descendants of Ishmael. Why Abelard should have done this raises an interesting question and it has been suggested that he modeled the Philosopher on a contemporary rationalist Mohammedan Ibn Badja (Avempace to the Latins) with whose reputation he had been acquainted by Peter the Venerable during his stay at Cluny. If the *Dialogue* was written before this time, however, Jolivet's suggestion demands some modification; see J. Jolivet, "Abélard et le philosophe (Occident et Islam au xiie siècle)," *Revue de l'histoire des religions* 164 (1963) 181-189, and R. Roques, "Les *pagani* dans le *Cur Deus homo* de Saint Anselm," ed. P. Wilpert, *Miscellanea Mediaevalia*, Bd. 2. *Die Metaphysik im Mittelalter. Ihr Ursprung und ihre Bedeutung*, Vorträge des ii. internationalen Kongresses für mittelalterliche Philosophie (Berlin, 1963), p. 199.

of men to be his own people, and why did he give the Law by which we would become holy, if only the joys of the present life – which the reprobate possess more than the chosen – were owing for the added observance of the Law ?

If holiness gains blessed and immortal life for your souls or for the souls of any men, it is clear that this is particularly owed to us also because of the Law, if its observance sanctifies us. And indeed it does sanctify, as the Lord himself says when speaking to us through Moses: "Therefore, if you hearken to my voice and keep my covenant, you shall be my special possession, dearer to me than all other people, for all the earth is mine. And you shall be to me a kingdom of priests, a holy nation."[71] So how did he choose us as his own people, and how does he sanctify us through the Law, if he makes you or others more blessed?

And further on when he was exhorting us to obey the Law, he says: "I am your God, bestowing mercy down to the thousandth generation on those who love me and keep my commandments."[72] What does "bestowing mercy down to the thousandth generation" mean except bestowing perfect and consummate mercy beyond which none can be extended, just as there are no new names for numbers beyond the thousands? In another place he says: "Be holy, for I, the Lord, your God, am holy."[73] Again: "Sanctify yourselves, and be holy; for I, the Lord, your God, am holy. Keep my commandments and carry them out. I am the Lord who makes you holy."[74] And further on: "To me you shall be sacred; for I, the Lord, am sacred, and

[71] Ex 19. 5-6.
[72] Ex 20. 5-6.
[73] Lv 19. 2.
[74] Lv 20. 7-8.

I have set you apart from the other nations to be my own."[75] And again: "It is I, the Lord, who makes you sacred and who led you out of the land of Egypt, that I might be your God."[76] Again: "If you live in accordance with my precepts I will set my tabernacle among you, and my soul will not disdain you."[77] In another place he says: "Who shall give them to have such a mind, to fear me and to keep all my commandments at all times, that it may be well with them and with their children forever"[78]

See, the Lord clearly proposes an everlasting reward for obedience to the Law, not a reward which comes to an end. And Moses, after the earthly reward for those who keep the Law, which you recalled above, added besides, that they will be filled with mercy by God, clearly promising to us a reward other than an earthly reward. When he began with, "it will be well with you all the days of your life as it is today," he immediately added: "and he will be merciful to us, if we keep and do all his precepts as he commanded us."[79] And somewhat further, when he said, "The Lord has chosen you from all the nations to be a people peculiarly his own"[80] he added: "Understand, then, that the Lord your God is a strong and faithful God who keeps his covenant and mercy down to the thousandth generation toward those who love him and keep his commandments."[81]

[75] Lv 20, 26.
[76] Lv 22, 32-33.
[77] Lv 26, 3.11.
[78] Dt 5, 29.
[79] See Dt 6, 24-25.
[80] Dt 7, 6.
[81] Dt 7, 9.

And I believe you are not ignorant of the fact that the Law itself commands the perfect love of God and neighbor which you claim comprises the natural law. In fact, when completing the Law at the end of his life, Moses says:

> And now, Israel, what does the Lord, your God, ask of you but to fear the Lord, your God, and follow his ways, and to love and serve the Lord, your God, with all your heart and all your soul, to keep the commandments and statutes of the Lord which I enjoin on you today for your own good? Think! The heavens, even the highest heavens, belong to the Lord, your God, the earth and everything on it. Yet in his love for your fathers the Lord was so attached to them as to choose you, their descendants, in preference to all other peoples, as this day it is proved.[82]

Indeed, the Law carefully makes the point that the love of God is to be perfect and it expands on it so far as to command that God is to be loved with our whole heart and our whole soul and with all our strength.[83] We are commanded to love our neighbor as ourselves, so that clearly the love of God, which is even extended beyond us, has no limits.[84] We are also commanded to love the very foreigners who live among us as ourselves, and the Law itself extends the embrace of love so far

---

[82] Dt 10, 12-15.

[83] See Dt 6, 5.

[84] Abelard quite explicitly denies that the Law of Moses recommends the love of neighbor if "neighbor" is understood to embrace all men. He points out that the Law distinguishes between neighbor and foreigner in Dt 23, 21; see Abelard, *Problemata Heloissae* 15 (PL. 178: 703c), and *Comm. Rom.* 4, CC.CM 11: 288. See also "But if we carefully examine the words of the Law, the Law never extends the term 'neighbor' except to men of its own people, that is, to the Jewish people" (*Comm. Rom.* 3, CC.CM 11: 191).

that its benefits are not to be lacking to our very enemies and to those who harm us.[85] Let us now offer a few [texts] in this regard:

> When you come upon your enemy's ox or ass going astray, bring it back to him. When you notice the ass of one who hates you lying prostrate under its burden, do not pass by, but help him to raise it up. You shall not oppress an alien since you were once aliens yourselves in the land of Egypt.[86]
>
> Take no revenge and cherish no grudge against your fellow countrymen. When an alien resides with you in your land, do not molest him. But let him be among you as a native; have the same love for him as for yourselves; for you too were once aliens in the land of Egypt. I, the Lord, am your God.[87]

And in another place:

> The needy will never be lacking in the land; that is why I command you to open your hand to your poor and needy kinsmen who live with you in the land.[88]

On the basis of these [texts] I ask you to consider how far the Law extends the affection of love to men as well as to God, so that you may recognise that even your law, which you call natural, is included in ours; and that even if the other precepts were to cease, these, which are the precepts of perfect love, would be sufficient both for our salvation and for yours. You

---

[85] See Lv 19, 18. Abelard himself explicitly denies that the Law of Moses commands the love of an enemy, but he allows that it does command the love of friends: "In fact, the Law of Moses never commands that the enemy be loved..."; *Problemata Heloissae* 15 (PL. 178: 703c).

[86] Ex 23, 4.5.9.

[87] Lv 19, 18.33-34.

[88] Dt 15, 11.

do not deny that our forefathers were saved by these, so that the security of salvation is all the more firmly bequeathed to us the more the other added precepts of the Law make life more constrained for us. And indeed it seems to me that this addition is not so much in the interests of respect for holy customs as to render this respect safer and more secure.

True love of God and men is sufficient for every virtue of the spirit, and if works should be lacking, nonetheless, a good and perfect will would never be diminished in its merit. But just as the Lord wished to separate us geographically from unbelievers lest we be corrupted through them, so he decreed that this be accomplished by means of ritual acts, as I said. Therefore, although the perfection of love is enough to merit true beatitude, certainly the additional precepts of a more constrained life ought to have gained something additional in this life at least, so that by the assurance of earthly benefits we would also become more prompt and secure in the service of God. And since his gifts to us would be increased, our devotion towards him would grow, and the outside population of unbelievers who would see this would be attracted more readily to the worship of God because of our benefits.

As to the point that the Lord seems to mention earthly benefits as the reward for observing the Law more often or more explicitly than eternal benefits, you should understand that this was done particularly because of a people as yet carnal and rebellious which he was leading to a severe solitude from the luxury of Egypt about which they were constantly murmuring. And it seemed superfluous to mention in the promise anything about eternal beatitude which, it was clear, the earlier fathers had received beforehand even without the handing on of the Law.

Finally, gather how perfect the Law is from this one measure which Moses writes down at the end of his life in these words: "And now, Israel, hear the commandments and decrees which I am teaching you, etc. You shall not add to the word that I speak to you, nor subtract from it."[89] And again: "Every command that I enjoin on you, that only do for the Lord, neither adding nor subtracting anything."[90] Surely, that is perfect to which nothing has to be added. But if any perfection were lacking, this prohibition would be evil which forbids the addition of what is lacking, and it blocks the road to beatitude for us. And why does the Law also command some things to be done through sacrifices and other observances for our purification or cleansing and for the forgiveness of sins, if this contributes nothing to true beatitude? Surely nothing excludes from true beatitude those whose sins are forgiven; otherwise you must not hope for it either. And why does he forbid us in the Law from sinning, unless he reserves for us what the absence of sin confers, and what its presence obstructs?

PHILOSOPHER: I am amazed that you, who are skilled in the Law, speak so rashly in extolling circumcision that you are not ashamed of lying when you say that God is only called the God of men after circumcision and not before, and only of those who were then circumcised, when for instance, he is called the God of Abraham and Isaac and Jacob. The written Law clearly refutes you when Noah said long before: "Blessed be the Lord,

[89] Dt 4, 1-2.
[90] Dt 13, 1.

the God of Shem; let Canaan be his slave."[91] See, Noah even calls God the God of Shem. So when "the God of Abraham, the God of Isaac, or of Jacob" is said, it is customary and not improper that the phrase, "and the God of our fathers," be added.

And if you even consider the divine benefits in which you particularly glory as if you were his own people, see that Enoch was happier when taken into paradise than you when led into the land of Canaan; and he is reported to have merited this when it is said: "And Enoch walked with God, and he was seen no more, for God took him."[92] On the other hand, Moses completely denies that you obtained the land of Canaan through your merits, saying: "After the Lord has thrust them out of your way, do not say to yourselves: For my justice he brought me in to possess this land. For it is really because of the wickedness of these nations that they are destroyed, in order to keep the promise which he made on oath to your fathers. Understand, therefore, it is not because of your merits that the Lord is giving you this good land, for you are a very stiff-necked people."[93]

After all men were destroyed except those of his own household, Noah indeed was made lord of what is on the earth and in the sea on account of his justice, and was allowed everything except blood for food.[94] Consequently, as regards the earthly benefits of God which you desire, the life of the earlier believers was happier to the extent that it was freer and master over all creatures of this earthly habitation. Moreover, just as

[91] Gn 9, 26.
[92] Gn 5, 24.
[93] Dt 9, 4-6.
[94] See Gn 9, 3-4.

the life of Noah and his household was freer than yours since it was not yet oppressed under the yoke of your Law, so our life is all the freer – that more ancient life which you are unable to prove is fettered by any external works of that harsh Law.

Indeed, let us carefully consider these works which began with Noah himself for whom the earlier law was established concerning abstinence from blood. And I knew some precepts of the Law were extended even to aliens, but only to those born in your household or to slaves or to those living within your gates or in your land with you. Scripture, indeed, carefully determines who these are in many passages, and you yourself have pointed them out above in citing the precept of the Law which provides for them to be treated mercifully just as native people. The Law assimilates them to you in many observances and clearly distinguishes them from other foreign travellers.[95] So when it says somewhere

> At the end of every seven-year period you shall have a relaxation of debts which shall be observed as follows. Every creditor shall relax his claim on what he has loaned his friend or neighbor or brother because it is the year of relaxation in honor of the Lord. Of the foreigner and stranger you may exact it,[96]

it clearly teaches that the stranger and the foreigner are not to be treated with the mercy with which a native person is to be

---

[95] The following discussion turns around four Latin words which can all mean "foreigner" or "stranger" – "alienigena," "advena," "alienus," "peregrinus." The scriptural texts follow the translation of the *New American Bible* (1970) which does not always reflect a consistent translation of the Latin terms. Abelard's basic distinction is between resident aliens and strangers who are just passing through. I have translated "alienigena" and "alienus" as "alien," "advena" as "foreigner" and "peregrinus" as "stranger."

[96] Dt 15, 1-3.

treated. It had also meant this stranger where it says: "All that is clean you shall eat. You must not eat any animal that had died of itself; give it to an alien who is within your gates and he may eat it, or sell it to him, for you are a people sacred to the Lord, your God."[97] And in another Book, at a time long before and in a passage similar to the above, the Law recommends that a foreigner who lives among you and who is not just passing through, not eat an animal which died of natural causes, just as it forbids you, saying: "The soul, whether a native or an alien, who eats of an animal that died of itself or was killed by a wild beast, shall wash his garments, bathe in water, and be unclean until evening, and then he will be clean. If he does not wash his garments and his body, he shall have the guilt to bear."[98]

Indeed, the man it calls a stranger and foreigner in one place, it sometimes calls an alien elsewhere, as when it is said: "You shall not demand interest from your countryman on a loan of money or of food or of anything else, but you may demand it from a foreigner."[99] However, in another place it is written of these foreigners who travel among you but not you among them: "If anyone, whether of the house of Israel or of the aliens that sojourn among you, partakes of any blood I will set my self against his soul and will cut him off from among his people."[100] In fact, in the precept of the Law you see that no other foreigner is to be understood than the one who lives among you and for this reason he is subject to your rule and

---

[97] Dt 14, 20-21.
[98] Lv 17, 15-16.
[99] Dt 23, 20.
[100] Lv 17, 10.

discipline. So with divine grace providing for us, a grace which has totally deprived you of any promise of a land, so that clearly no one journeys among you but you journey among all peoples, you should know that we are not obliged to any of your legal observances.

You try to urge us to circumcision on the basis of the precept of circumcision and the example of Abraham. As a result you would also include in the sacrament of the Law those to whom, you agree, no Law was given; nor is the promise of the land made to them which was laid down in the covenant of circumcision. Consider how groundless your objection is. For when the Lord first said, "Every male from among you shall be circumcised" and added, "Every male in your generations both the houseborn slave and the slave acquired with money and whoever is not of your blood," surely by "from among you" he understands not only Abraham and his descendants, but those besides who belong to their family or possessions so that they had the power to order and compel them to be circumcised. Consequently, after he said, "from among you" and afterwards added, "in your generations, both the houseborn slave and the slave acquired with money," finally he added, "whoever is not of your blood." By "in your generations" and "whoever is not of your blood" he carefully expressed what he had meant above when he said "from among you," that is, not only the generations of their descendants but also the families of aliens which they possess.

Similarly when he says "and my covenant will be in your flesh," this expression "in your flesh" is to be taken in a general sense like the previous expression, "among you." Otherwise the promise would have been very incongruous, as if God's covenant does not appear in their flesh unless foreigners were also circumcised just as the others. So it is clear that by the expression, "in your flesh," foreigners are also to be understood. What is added at the end also completes the view: "A male, if the flesh of his foreskin is not circumcised, that soul will perish out of his people since he makes my covenant worthless." How is this passage to be reconciled with the previous in which foreigners were already understood unless his covenant is also with foreigners, at least when it is said, "circumcised from among you, etc."?

Your efforts to show that the eternal beatitude of souls was also promised to you through your legal prescriptions can be shown, on the basis of the Law itself, to be the worst sort of guessing. In fact, you understand by the expression "with an eternal covenant" or "for an eternal covenant" that those who will be circumcised according to the precept of God are so covenanted with him forever that they will not be separated from his grace in the future. So there must be absolutely no doubt that Ishmael or Esau or most of those who were outcasts must be saved. I am surprised you do not notice that "eternal" or "everlasting" are frequently understood in the Law in such a way as to refer to nothing beyond the duration of the present life. So even when it is first said in the very covenant of circumcision, "I will give to you and to your descendants the land in which you are now staying, the whole land of Canaan, as an eternal possession,"[101] I do not believe you are so stupid as to include in the term "eternal" the blessedness of a future life for which it was out of place here to provide any teaching. As you know, in those works of the Law which were only

---

[101] Gn 17, 8.

celebrated in this life, the Law is often accustomed to add the expression, "this will be an everlasting statute for you and for all your generations and households." For, to take one example from among many, it makes this addition in the case of the celebration of the festival of Tabernacles. When it first said, "On the first day you shall gather the fruits of the fairest tree and branches of palms and boughs covered with leaves and willows of the brook and then you shall make merry before the Lord, your God. And you shall keep the solemnity thereof seven days in the year," it immediately added: "It shall be a perpetual statute for you and your descendants." [102]

When instituting the celebration of the Sabbath on the seventh day he says somewhere, "It is a perpetual covenant, between me and the children of Israel and an everlasting token." [103] And when the Lord says of the Hebrew slave who does not wish to depart as a free man, that he will be a slave forever, [104] he means only the duration of his life, for according to the Law Hebrew slaves are not passed on to posterity as is the case for slaves who were taken from other peoples. Hence it is written:

> Slaves, male and female, you may possess, provided you buy them from among the aliens who reside with you and from their children who are born in your land. These slaves you may own and leave to your posterity as their hereditary property, and possess them forever. But you shall not lord it harshly over your kinsmen, the sons of Israel. [105]

[102] Lv 23, 40-41.
[103] Ex 31, 16-17.
[104] See Ex 21, 5-6.
[105] Lv 25, 44-46.

It was surely sufficient for the Lord, in rewarding such a carnal people who knew only earthly things, to adapt the reward to this present life alone.

While commending the perfection of the Law you claimed that only what Moses commanded must be done. I am surprised that you have forgotten what you yourself claimed before when you said that it was praiseworthy that many additions were made to the precepts out of concern for you, and everyone knows that this is clearly most true. Whence you have received some traditions of the fathers subsequent to the Law which you judge to be most useful. For instance, following the example of Daniel who refused the royal food and wine lest he be defiled by it, you also abstain from our wine.[106] And even the Rechabites, by abstaining from wine forever on the command of Jonadab their father, went beyond the precepts of Moses as well as the traditions of all your fathers. Jeremiah, who was sent to them by the Lord to offer them wine to drink, was not even given a hearing by them. Consequently, the Lord so praised their obedience that he made them this promise, saying: "Since you have obeyed the command of Jonadab, your father, and have kept all his commands, never shall there fail to be a descendant of Jonadab, Recheb's son, standing in my service."[107] Was King Hezekiah a transgressor of the Law when he broke the bronze serpent; was not this destruction, which was done without a command, praiseworthy, just as its construction on command had been useful?[108]

---

[106] See Dn 1, 8.
[107] Jer 35, 18-19.
[108] See 2 Kgs 18, 4; Nm 21, 9.

And when David composed the psalms in God's honor, or when he solemnly led the ark of the Lord to Jerusalem,[109] or when Solomon constructed and dedicated the temple of the Lord,[110] they surely did what Moses had in no way commanded. Furthermore, all the prophets were called without a precept from Moses or of the Law which was given to him. The holy fathers did innumerable things after Moses either on the command of the Lord or for clear utility which are in no way contained in the precepts of Moses.

For the Lord's precepts must not be expected in those things having a clear utility; nor is it sinful to do what is not prescribed, but it is sinful to act contrary to a precept. Otherwise you would not be able to get through any day of the present life nor look after domestic cares, since we have to do many things such as buying, conducting business, travelling from one place to another, or even eating or sleeping, which are not governed by any precept. Furthermore, who does not see that if one must not do more or less than Moses commanded, all who keep the Law are equal in merit, not one better than the other among those whose merits cannot be unequal. So it is clear from the foregoing that you can in no way commend the perfection of the Law by understanding that something is contrary to the Law if it is added to it but not prescribed in it.

And you should recognize that you do not satisfactorily justify the Lord's passing over the highest reward when recommending obedience to the Law, if he judged this obedience sufficient to merit that reward too, as I said.

[109] 2 Sm 6.
[110] 1 Kgs 6.

I am surprised that you are confident that spiritual good is obtained from the purification of sins through sacrifices or any external works of the Law, if, as you yourself profess and it is evident, your love of God and neighbor is enough for the justification of holiness. For without this love the external works are of no benefit for the salvation of the soul, nor is there any doubt that when love has made anyone just there is then no guilt of sin in him which needs spiritual purification. This is why your Scripture speaks as it does of the repentant sinner: "A sacrifice to God is a contrite spirit, etc."[111] And again: "I said: I will confess against myself my injustice and you took away the guilt of my sin."[112] See how it commends this sacrifice of a contrite heart, while elsewhere, in the person of the Lord, it completely rejects what is external, saying:

> Hear, O people, and I will speak; Israel, I take from your house no bullocks, no goats out of your fold. If I were hungry, I should not tell you, for mine are the world and its fullness. Shall I eat the flesh of strong bulls, or is the blood of goats my drink? Offer to God praise as your sacrifice and fulfill your vows to the Most High. Then call upon me in time of distress; I will rescue you, and you shall glorify me.[113]

The Lord hungers for the sacrifice of the heart, not the sacrifice of animals, and he is replenished by it. When he finds the former, he does not seek the latter; when he does not find it, the other is entirely worthless. I speak here of what concerns the justification of the soul, not the avoidance of legal penalties; yet your sins are said to be forgiven through these penalties.

[111] Ps 51, 19.
[112] Ps 32, 5.
[113] Ps 50, 7.9.12-15.

In fact, your Law which grants merits or demerits only in this life for fulfilling or transgressing it, and carries a reward in both cases only here, likewise adapts everything to this bodily life so that it judges nothing clean or unclean from the point of view of the soul, and it does not provide any purifications for the impurity of souls, which we call sins in the proper sense. Hence it calls food clean and unclean in the same way as men; and it frequently calls beds and chairs and all household ustensils and even clothing, and many other inanimate things unclean or polluted.[114] Now if you number the uncleanliness of men for whom purifications have been established with those who have been defiled by sins, are you going to judge the woman who was cleansed after childbirth by a sacrifice to have committed a sin just because she bore a child? Should you not rather judge her cursed who leaves no seed for Israel?

What sin does the man incur from suffering a flow of semen? But the Law considers him so abhorrent that the bed in which he sleeps and wherever he sits is unclean as a consequence. The earthen vase which he touches will be broken and the wooden one should be washed. If another touches his bed or sits where the unclean man had sat, that other will wash his clothes, and even when he has washed himself in water he will remain impure until evening. And a woman who suffers natural menstruation is considered to be so unclean that wherever she sleeps or sits is also so polluted that she pollutes everything by her touch, like the man mentioned above who suffers a flow of semen.

Why, I ask you, can contact with a bed be polluting in reference to the soul? What, I pray, is this uncleanliness or

---

[114] See Lv 15.

these pollutions? Certainly, they belong to the same class as
some foods, and just as these latter are forbidden you to eat, so
the former are forbidden you to touch; and as the latter are
unclean because they must not be eaten, so the former are
unclean or polluted because they must not be touched. And
those who touch these things, even under compulsion or
unknowingly, are likwise pronounced to be unclean since they
are forbidden the fellowship of conversation until the
prescribed end of the purification. But what are obvious sins,
such as murder or adultery and the like, are punished with
death rather than expiated through sacrifices. And the remedy
of such purifications is not granted to them whereby those who
committed the acts are able to be saved.

From this you should understand that these purifications are
more adapted to a certain respectability of this life than to the
salvation of the soul. And when the sins of such are said to be
forgiven it is clear that the corporeal punishments which were
instituted for them are mitigated for those who are separated
from the community. For can we understand the forgiveness
of sin otherwise than as the mitigation of the punishment due
it, whether the punishment be corporeal or perpetual?

The guilty man, in truth, is compromised by the decision of
his soul; through his contrite heart and genuine penitential
compunction, he is pardoned immediately in such a way that
he is no longer at any disadvantage on that account, as was
said: "I said: I will confess against myself."[115] Once a penitent
sinner has decided to accuse himself by confessing, already by
this fact the fault of the perverse will by which he sinned is
then free of guilt and his perpetual punishment is remitted,
even though a temporal punishment might still be retained for

[115] Ps 32, 5.

the sake of his correction, as your Prophet elsewhere notes the same thing by saying: "Though the Lord has indeed chastised me, yet he has not delivered me to death."[116]

I think that in the inquiry into the matter of the salvation of my soul I have conferred with you enough on the subject of your faith or mine. Indeed, in considering our conversation, I think it has been settled that, even if you received it from God, you are able to know that I am not obliged on the authority of your Law to submit to its burden, as if something necessary were to be added to the law which Job prescribes for us by his example, or to the discipline of morals which our philosophers left to posterity in what concerns the virtues, which are sufficient for beatitude. Now it remains to hear the decision of the present judge on this matter, or it remains for me to shift the efforts of our inquiry to the Christian.

(Judge): Both agree to receive the decision of our judgment. I, however, more desirous of learning than of judging, answer that I wish first to hear the arguments of all so that the wiser I become by listening, the more discerning will I be in judging, in the spirit of what I recalled above according to a proverb of the wisest of men: "A wise man by learning will be wiser, an intelligent man will gain sound guidance."[117] All unanimously agreed to this, inflamed with the same desire to learn.[118]

[116] Ps 118, 18.
[117] Prv 1, 5.
[118] "The first conference of the Philosopher with the Jew ends. The second of the same with the Christian begins." Added in Oxford, Balliol College MS 296, fol. 170v. Notice that this paragraph is a narrative account and not a direct speech. I have placed the word "judge" in brackets since no one is actually speaking; the word is omitted in the Oxford, Balliol MS and Thomas says it is written in the margin of the Vienna MS by a second hand, see *Dialogus*, ed. R. Thomas, at line 1165.

<The Philosopher
and the Christian>

PHILOSOPHER: So now I address you, O Christian, that you too might respond to my inquiry, in accordance with the terms of our plan. Indeed your law should be all the more perfect, more compelling in reward, and its teaching more reasonable, the more recent it is. The earlier laws would have surely been written in vain for the people unless something were added to them to perfect the teaching. Giving this careful consideration in the second Book of the *Rhetoric*, one of our own, when he gave an opinion on the question of contrary laws, laid down the rule that attention must be given to "which law was passed last, for the latest law is always the most important."[119]

CHRISTIAN: I am surprised that you are so shamelessly at variance with what you professed at the beginning. For although you first claimed that in your inquiries you had found the Jews to be stupid and the Christians insane, and afterwards you said you were not seeking verbal controversy, but meeting to inquire into the truth, why do you now finally expect the teaching of truth from those you even found to be insane? Do you think that now, after your inquiries, their insanity ceases to the point that they are able to suffice for your instruction?

[119] Cicero. *De inventione* 2.49.145.

Surely, if you think the Christian religious school of thought to be insane and consider those who follow it to be insane, consider, Philosopher, what must be thought of those outstanding Greek philosophers who were all converted to this school of thought by the rude and unlettered preaching of simple men, that is, by the preaching of the apostles, and who became the most insane.[120] And what you call our insanity was so rooted and established among the Greeks that it was there that the evangelical as well as the apostolic teaching was written and afterwards great councils held so that from there it filled the whole world and repressed all heresies.

PHILOSOPHER: Sometimes men are more easily challenged by loud abuses and taunts, than persuaded by prayers and offerings; and those who are challenged in this way are more zealously concerned with battle than those who are entreated and moved by a gracious approach.

CHRISTIAN: You must be pardoned if you did this with that intention. Now, lest I seem to avoid this battle out of a lack of confidence, let us both pray that the Lord, who wishes all men to be saved and to come to the knowledge of himself,[121] may inspire us, both as to what you should ask and as to what I should reply.

PHILOSOPHER: Amen.

---

[120] For the rustic and unlettered apostles see Sermon 19 (PL. 178: 515c-D) and Hymns 64 and 65 (PL. 178: 1805a-b).
[121] See 1 Tm 2, 4.

CHRISTIAN: All right. So now, if it is agreeable, since you have no share in the perfection of our Law, that is, in the evangelical and apostolic teaching, let us first inspect it and compare it with all other teachings so that if you find its exhortations and precepts which justify to be more perfect, you will choose it more readily, as is only proper. As you said, this is what your rhetorician recalls above; when considering contrary laws, his advice is: "If two laws or several cannot be kept because they are at variance, the one is thought to have the greatest claim to be upheld which has reference to the greatest matters."[122]

PHILOSOPHER: Nothing is more plausible than this advice, and nothing is more stupid than to abandon ancient laws for new ones except for those whose teaching is more compelling. Clearly, those who wrote these new laws were able to write them more carefully and more perfectly to the extent that, instructed in the discipline of the earlier laws and by the experience of contemporary necessities, they were easily able to add what was lacking through their own talent, as also happens in other philosophical disciplines. Then the greatest confidence must be placed in the ability of later writers, if the modern writers can equal the ancients in talent.

But what must be expected if they perhaps even far surpass them? You have no doubt that this is the case with Christ the legislator whom you call the very Wisdom of God. You even say that our Job praised him in these words in the past: "Behold God in his power and none is like him among the law-givers."[123] And your Apostle, showing a preference for his

---

[122] Cicero, *De inventione* 2.49.145.
[123] Jb 36, 22.

teaching and clearly acknowledging the imperfection of the first Law, says: "In times past God spoke in fragmentary and varied ways to our fathers through the prophets; in this, the final ages he has spoken to us through his Son, etc."[124] And further on, when distinguishing between the Old and the New Law, he again says: "The former commandment has been annulled because of its weakness and uselessness, for the law brought nothing to perfection. But a better hope has supervened, and through it we draw near to God."[125]

CHRISTIAN: Certainly, as I see it, ignorance of our faith does not condemn you but rather the obstinacy of your unbelief. You have learned about the perfection of our Law from its writings and still you ask what you should follow, as if you did not have there a perfect example – an example more excellent than all others – of the virtues which, you do not doubt, suffice for beatitude. Indeed, with his Old Testament complete, when the Lord himself handed down the New, he speaks to his disciples at the very beginning of this perfection which they lacked: "Unless your justice surpass, etc."[126] And going on immediately he carefully gave expression to the richness of the New Law through examples of what lacked moral perfection, and he brought a true ethics to perfection. Certainly in this comparison it will easily be shown that whatever had been handed down from the ancient fathers and from the prophets concerning the discipline of morals and the different virtues is as nothing if we carefully compare these with the more recent teachings.

[124] Heb 1, 1-2.
[125] Heb 7, 18-19.
[126] Mt 5, 20.

PHILOSOPHER: You know that only the desire of such comparisons drew me here, and we were all of us assembled with this intention.

CHRISTIAN: As far as I see, we are now actually making our way towards the goal and summit of all disciplines. What you call ethics, that is, moral discipline, we are accustomed to call divinity. Clearly, our name arises from what it is aimed at comprehending, that is, God, yours from those things through which it is attained there, that is, from good moral actions which you call virtues.

PHILOSOPHER: I agree that what you say is clear, and I give my wholehearted approval to your new usage. For, because you judge the point of arrival more worthy than the means of arrival and the arrival more blessed than the journey, yours is the naming of higher things and from the very etymology of the term, as from "divining," it more immediately draws the reader. If it is as preeminent on the force of evidence as the name suggests, I think that no discipline is comparable to it. So now, if it is agreeable, we wish you to outline a summary of the true ethics, and what we must contemplate through this discipline, and when it is reached, where its goal is realised.

CHRISTIAN: I think that a complete summary of this discipline is brought together in this: it should disclose where the supreme good is and by what route we are to arrive there.

PHILOSOPHER: It is surely most satisfying that a summary of such a great matter is expressed in so few words, and the goal of the whole of ethics is so precisely summed up. Indeed, this statement of the goal immediately draws the hearer to itself and recommends the study of this discipline, so that the teachings of all the arts become worthless in comparison with it. For, to the degree that the supreme good, in whose enjoyment true beatitude rests, is more excellent than all others, undoubtedly its study excels all others by far in usefulness as well as in worth. In fact, the studies of the other arts remain far below the supreme good, nor do they touch the height of beatitude; and there is no profit apparent in them except insofar as they serve this highest philosophy, like ladies-in-waiting who busy themselves around their mistress. For what value is there in the study of grammar or dialectic or the other arts for the investigation of man's true beatitude? All lie far below this eminence and are unable to raise themselves to such a height. But they do treat of certain ways of speaking or they are concerned with the natures of things as if preparing steps towards this height, since we must speak of it, and through the natures of things we are given examples or analogies. The result is that through them we get in touch with the mistress as if we had been introduced by her ladies-in-waiting, possessing the approach, indeed, thanks to them, whereas it is in her that we obtain rest and our fatigue comes to an end.[127]

[127] The same relationship between the sciences and theology is presented by Richard Fishacre in a passage which echoes this text of Abelard, see J. Long, "The Science of Theology according to Richard Fishacre: Edition of the Prologue to his *Commentary on the Sentences*," *Mediaeval Studies* 34 (1972) 85. On several occasions the Philosopher points out the role of reason and secular studies in relation to the study of the supreme good. In almost every case his words and the authorities he uses reflect positions of Abelard, Letter 13 (PL 178: 351-356).

CHRISTIAN: I am glad that you have so carefully touched upon the excellence of this philosophy and have distinguished it from the other arts. I understand from this that you are deeply occupied in its study.

PHILOSOPHER: I say "properly" occupied. In fact, this alone is the discipline of natural law which, being concerned with moral precepts, is all the more suited to philosophers the more it is evident that they use this law and adhere to reasons, as your own teacher recalls, saying: "For Jews demand 'signs' and Greeks look for 'wisdom'."[128] Surely, the Jews alone, since they are animals and sensual and are imbued with no philosophy whereby they are able to discuss reasoned arguments, are moved to faith only by the miracles of external deeds, as if it were the case that it belongs to God alone to effect these things and that no illusion could be produced in them by demons. The magicians in Egypt taught them, and Christ in particular instructed you, how stupid it is to accept this. Warning them about the false prophets of anti-Christ, he declared that such great miracles would be worked for the seduction of men, "as to mislead even the chosen if that were possible."[129]

Therefore, as if it were foolishness to seek these signs, the aforesaid Apostle reminds us of the opposite when he added, "And the Greeks look for wisdom," that is, they require reasons from preachers, which are the sure instruments of wisdom. Consequently, your preaching, that is, the Christian preaching, is most highly commended because it was able to

[128] 1 Cor 1, 22.
[129] Mt 24, 24.

convert to the faith those who were well grounded in and rich in reasons, namely, those who were imbued with the study of all the liberal arts and armed with reasons. Indeed, they were not only investigators in these studies, but also inventors, and from their fonts rivers flowed into the whole world. This is why we now have particular confidence in your discipline seeing that, the stronger and more established it has already grown, the more capable it is in rational debate.

CHRISTIAN: Yes indeed, after the conversion of such great philosophers, neither you nor your posterity can be in doubt about our faith; and there does not now seem to be any need for such a conflict as this. For why would you believe everything on their authority in the secular disciplines but not be moved to the faith by their example, saying with the Prophet: "For we are no better than our fathers."[130]

PHILOSOPHER: We do not accede to their authority in such a manner that we refuse to submit their words to rational scrutiny before we give our assent. Otherwise we would stop philosophizing if, for instance, neglecting the examination of reasons, we were to make greater use of arguments from authority. These are understood to be devoid of intellectual creativity and totally separated from the matter itself, resting on opinion rather than on truth. Moreover, we should not believe that our ancestors were led to the confession of your faith so much by reason as that they were dragged by force, as your own histories agree. In fact, before the conversion to your faith of emperors or princes through miracles, as you say, your

[130] See 1 Kgs 19, 4.

preaching won over few or no wise men, although the people could then be easily torn from the most obvious errors of idolatry and converted to any cult of the one God. Whence your own Paul, on the occasion of his invective against the Athenians, prudently says at the beginning, "Men of Athens, I see that in every respect you are superstitious, etc."[131] For by then the knowledge of natural law and of divine worship had disappeared and a multitude of those in error had entirely destroyed or oppressed the few who were wise. But to speak from our conscience and to give its due to the not unimportant fruit of Christian preaching, we do not doubt that through it idolatry was then largely destroyed in the world.

CHRISTIAN: Add that it is also clear that natural law was revived and the perfect discipline of morals, on which alone you say you base yourself and which you believe suffices for salvation, was handed on by him alone; and whoever were instructed by him as by true wisdom, that is the wisdom of God, must be called true philosophers.[132]

PHILOSOPHER: And would that you could clearly prove what you say and that through the supreme wisdom itself which you call in Greek *logos* and in Latin *verbum Dei*, you might show yourselves true logicians and armed with reasons to go with your words! You should not presume that I will allege as an excuse that saying of your Gregory, that miserable refuge: "Faith has no merit for which human reason offers proof."[133]

---

[131] Acts 17, 22.
[132] See Abelard, Letter 13 (PL 178: 355c).
[133] Gregory the Great, *Homiliae XL in Evangelia* 26.1 (PL 76: 1197). For

Because your people are not able to discuss the faith which they affirm, they immediately take up this phrase of Gregory as solace for their lack of skill. Indeed, in their opinion what else does this mean but that we should assent to the faith on the grounds of any sort of preaching, whether stupid or reasonable? For if, through fear of losing merit, faith rules out all rational discussion and there is no room for judgment in the discussion of what ought to be believed, but instant assent must be given to what is preached whatever the errors sown by this preaching, acceptance has no point because there is no room for rational refutation where the use of reason is not permitted. Let an idolater say of stone or wood or any creature, "Here is the true God, creator of heaven and earth," or let him preach any clear abomination; who would be able to refute him, if there is to be no rational discussion of the faith?[134] He will immediately use against his critic, particularly if the critic is a Christian, what was already said: "Faith has no merit, etc." The Christian will straightway be thrown into confusion by his own defense, saying as he does that his reasons ought to have absolutely no hearing in matters such as these – where the Christian absolutely forbids that they be introduced, neither can he justifiably attack anyone on a matter of faith by adducing reasons, since he permits no one to attack him with reasons.

Abelard's use of this text see E. Buytaert, "Abelard's *Collationes*," *Antonianum* 44 (1969) 25, and R. Thomas, *Der philosophisch-theologische Erkenntnisweg Peter Abaelards im 'Dialogus inter Philosophum, Iudaeum et Christianum'*, Untersuchungen zur allgemeinen Religionsgeschichte, Neue Folge 6 (Bonn, 1966), pp. 76-80.

[134] See Abelard, *Theologia 'Scholarium'* 2.3 (PL. 178: 1050B-D).

CHRISTIAN: As that greatest of wise men says, "Sometimes a way seems right to a man, but the end of it leads to death."[135] Likewise, what often seem to be reasons, that is, reasonable and appropriate statements, are not so at all.

PHILOSOPHER: And what about those which are taken for authorities? Is there not often error in them? Otherwise there would not be so many diverse religious schools of thought, if all were to use the same authorities. But just as each deliberates using his own reason, each and all choose the authorities they follow. Moreover, the opinions expressed in all writings would have to be received indifferently if reason, which is naturally prior to them, did not have the right to judge them first. For those who wrote thanks only to reason – with which their opinions seem to abound – merited authority, that is, worth with respect to belief as an immediate consequence. However, in their judgment reason is also preferred to authority to such a degree that, as your own Anthony also recalls: "Since the insight of human reason was the source of writings, for the person in whom the insight is sound, there is no need of writings."[136]

---

[135] Prv 14, 12.

[136] Athanasius, *Vita beati Antonii, interprete Evagrio* 45 (PL 73: 158); English translation: R. T. Meyer, *St. Athanasius. The Life of Saint Anthony*, Ancient Christian Writers, 10 (Westminster, Maryland, 1950), Ch. 73. John Scottus Eriugena had written: "For authority proceeds from true reason, but reason certainly does not proceed from authority. For every authority which is not upheld by true reason is seen to be weak, whereas true reason is kept firm and immutable by her own powers and does not require to be confirmed by the assent of any authority. For it seems to me that true authority is nothing else but the truth that has been discovered by the power of reason and set down in writing by the Holy Fathers for the use of posterity." *Periphyseon (De divisione naturae) liber primus*, ed. and tr. I. P.

In every philosophical disputation authority is thought so to hold last place or no place at all that it is utterly shameful for those who trust in their own powers and scorn the refuge of another's wealth to introduce arguments which are based on extrinsic judgment, that is, on authority. When the orator more than the philosopher is compelled to seek refuge in them, philosophers have rightfully judged the topics of such arguments to be totally extrinsic, dissociated from the facts, and destitute of all strength. This is because they rest on opinion rather than on truth and make no use of intelligence in building up their arguments, since the one who introduces them uses not his own words but the words of others. So your own Boethius in his *Topics*, while explaining the division of topics of both Themistius and Tully, says, "'Extrinsic judgment': that is, arguments which present testimony, as it were, and are topics without creative intelligence and are entirely disjunctive, following judgment and opinion and not based on the reality itself."[137] Again Boethius, when speaking of Tully's

---

Sheldon-Williams with the collaboration of Ludwig Bieler in Scriptores latini Hiberniae, 7 (Dublin, 1968), p. 199. See Honorius of Autun, *Libellus octo quaestionum* 1 (PL 172: 1185), and for a discussion of the concept of authority in the Middle Ages, see M. D. Chenu, *La théologie au douzième siècle*, chapter 16.

[137] Boethius, *De differentiis topicis* 2 (PL 64: 1195A). For "*inartificialis*" = "without creative intelligence" see Boethius, *In Topica Ciceronis commentaria* 2 (PL 64: 1082B) and Cicero, *Topica* 4.24, tr. H. M. Hubbell, The Loeb Classical Library (Cambridge, Mass., 1949). The Philosopher is here discussing one of the topics or sources of argument known as the argument from authority. A topic or *locus* is a source for the inferential strength of an argument; see Abelard, *Dialectica*, First complete edition of the Parisian manuscript, 2nd rev. edition, ed. L. M. De Rijk (Assen, 1970), p. 253 and pp. 438-439. See O. Bird, "The Tradition of the Logical Topics: Aristotle to Ockham," *Journal of the History of Ideas* 23 (1962), 307-323.

treatment of the same topic, says: "That topic remains which, he said, is drawn from the outside. It is based on judgment and authority and completely probable, containing no element of necessity."[138] And further on he says: "This topic is truly said to be extrinsically constituted since it is not understood in relation to the subject or predicate terms but it comes from outside after a judgment has been made. Hence he says that it is said to be devoid of creative intelligence and artless, since the orator does not construct the argument for himself but uses testimonies already prepared and established."[139]

What you said about the possibility of error in the discernmet or knowledge of reasons is true and obvious, but this happens with those men who lack the skill of rational philosophy and the capacity for distinguishing arguments.[140] The Jews who require signs in place of arguments acknowledge themselves to be of this sort; and it is the same for those who place their defense in the words of another. It is as if the authority or writing of a person who is absent were judged more easily than the reason or opinion of a person who is present, and as if the meaning of the former could be inquired into better than that of the latter.

When, concerned for our salvation, we inquire after God to the best of our ability, his grace surely makes up for what our efforts do not furnish, and he aids those who are willing so that they might have the ability, and he even inspires them with the will.[141] And he who often draws the unwilling does not reject

---

[138] Boethius, *De diff. top.* 3 (PL. 64: 1199c).
[139] Boethius, *De diff. top.* 3 (PL. 64: 1199d).
[140] See Abelard, Letter 13 (PL. 178: 356c).
[141] See Phil 2, 13, and Abelard, Sermon 5 (PL. 178: 425a).

the willing, and he stretches his right hand to the one who is struggling and whose negligence he cannot reprove. In this regard Christ, whom you call Truth itself, to make you secure, added at the end of an apt parable: "Ask, and you will receive. Seek, and you will find. Knock, and it will be opened to you. For the one who asks, receives; and the one who seeks, finds; and to him who knocks, it will be opened."[142] As I recall, when commenting on these words in one of his writings entitled *On Mercy* Augustine says, "Ask by praying, seek by disputation, knock by requesting."[143] Whence, in the second Book of *On Order*, placing the art of disputation before the other disciplines as if it alone has knowledge or makes knowers, he recommends it in these words: "The discipline of disciplines which they call 'dialectic'. This teaches both how to teach and how to learn. In it reason exhibits itself, and it alone knows what it is and what it wants. It not only wants to make us knowers but is able to do so."[144]

Likewise, in the second Book of *On Christian Doctrine*, showing that it is absolutely necessary for the reading of Scripture, he says:

> There remain those institutions which do not pertain to the corporeal senses but to the reason, where the sciences of disputation and number hold sway. The science of disputation is of great value for understanding and solving all sorts of questions that appear in sacred literature. However, in this

---

[142] Mt 7, 7-8.

[143] See (Pseudo-)Augustine, *Tractatus de oratione et eleemosyna* (PL 40: 1227), and E. Buytaert, "Abelard's *Collationes*." p. 24, n. 21.

[144] Augustine, *On Order* 2.13.38, tr. R. P. Russell, *Divine Providence and the Problem of Evil*, in The Fathers of The Church, 1 (New York, 1948), p. 315. See Abelard, Letter 13 (PL 178: 353c).

connection the love of controversy is to be avoided, as well as a certain puerile ostentation in deceiving an adversary. There are, moreover, many false conclusions of the reasoning process called sophisms, and frequently they so imitate true conclusions that they mislead not only those who are slow but also the ingenious when they do not pay close attention. As I see it, the Scripture condemns this kind of captious conclusion in that place where it is said, "He that speaketh sophistically is hateful."[145]

CHRISTIAN: Certainly, no one in his senses would forbid rational investigation and discussion of our faith, nor is there any reasonable assenting to what is doubtful before having a rational basis for doing so. For example, when reason believes in something doubtful, surely it does so by what you call an argument. In fact, in every discipline controversy arises in regard to the written word as well as in regard to the opinions expressed,[146] and in any disputation the giving of a reason is firmer than a display of authority. The question of what is really the truth is not an issue for the building up of the faith, but rather it is a question of what can be held by opinion; and many questions arise concerning the words of the authority itself, so that judgment must be rendered on them before it is

[145] Augustine, *On Christian Doctrine* 2.31.48, tr. D. W. Robertson Jr., in The Library of Liberal Arts (Indianapolis, Indiana, 1958), p. 67; internal reference to Sir 37, 23 (Vulgate); see Abelard, Letter 13 (PL 178; 353D), and *Dialectica* 4, ed. L. De Rijk; 2nd ed., p. 470 for Abelard's praise of dialectic.

[146] See Cicero, *De inventione* 1.40.116 and [Cicero] *Ad C. Herennium. De ratione dicendi (Rhetorica ad Herennium)* 4.1.11.19, tr. H. Caplan, The Loeb Classical Library (Cambridge, Mass., 1954); Abelard, *Theol. christ.* 2.136 and 3.1, CC.CM 12: 138 and 194.

rendered by means of them.[147] After reasonable judgment has been rendered, even if the solution is not rationally conclusive but appears so, no further question remains since there is no doubt left.

Certainly, with you there is all the less cause for an appeal to authority the more you use the support of reason and the less you acknowledge the authority of Scripture. Indeed, no one can be shown the truth except on the basis of what he already admits, nor is he to be refuted except on the basis of what he accepts; but it is one thing to enter into conflict with you and another to do so among ourselves. What Gregory or our other teachers or even Christ himself or Moses said, we knew did not yet pertain to you, in the sense that through their words you would be compelled to the faith. Among ourselves who accept these they have a place. But above all, the faith must sometimes be built up or defended by reasons. Of these reasons – I recall against those who deny that the faith must be subject to rational investigation – the second Book of *Christian Theology* fully discourses with the power of reasons as well as with the authority of Scripture, and it does successfully refute opponents.[148] Now, if it is agreeable, let us return to our plan.

PHILOSOPHER: Yes, indeed, because it is agreeable; and it must be agreeable above all to give our best effort, and we are compelled to seek the natural law in the testimony of a more

[147] Abelard's 'Prologue' to the *Sic et Non* is concerned with the problems which the use of authorities encounters and he suggests there how these problems might be resolved. For an English translation of this Prologue see, eds. B. Polka and B. Zelechow, *Readings in Western Civilization*, Vol. 1. *The Intellectual Adventure of Man to 1600* (Toronto, 1970), pp. 102-114.

[148] Abelard, *Theol. chris.* 2, CC.CM 12: 132-193.

authentic ethics.[149] We believe this will come to a proper and orderly conclusion if we discuss what the supreme good is, and by what route it must be attained there, according to the comprehensive summary of ethics which you gave above. Consequently, the treatise of our ethics is divided into two parts in these matters.

CHRISTIAN: I agree with your recommendation. But because our views are to be compared with yours according to the conditions of the above proposal in order for us to be able to choose the more compelling, and since your have claimed first place for yourself because of the antiquity of the natural law, it is yours. As you say, you are satisfied with the first, that is, the natural law, and use only it. Present your opinions or those of your people, and afterwards, if we disagree in something, listen to the reasons for our opinions.

PHILOSOPHER: They define the supreme good or the goal of the good, that is, its consummation or perfection, as most of your own remind us, in this way: "that which, when attained, makes one blessed";[150] and on the other hand, the supreme evil they define in this way: that whose possession makes one wretched. And we merit both through moral actions. However, it is well known that moral actions are called virtues or their contraries vices.[151] But some of us, as Augustine

---

[149] See Abelard, *Theol. christ.* 2.44, CC.CM 12: 149.

[150] Augustine, *The City of God* 8.3, trs. G. G. Walsh and G. Monahan, *The City of God.* Books VIII-XVI, The Fathers of the Church, 14 (New York, 1952), p. 26.

[151] See Abelard, *Ethics*, ed. D. E. Luscombe, p. 3.

reminds us in the eighth Book of *The City of God*, said that virtue itself is the supreme good, others that pleasure is.[152]

CHRISTIAN: And what, I pray, did they understand pleasure to be?

PHILOSOPHER: Not, as many think, the immorality of carnal enticements and base amusement, but a certain interior peace of soul by which it remains at rest and content with its own goods in the midst of adversity and prosperity, while no consciousness of sin gnaws at it.[153] For it is unthinkable that philosophers, who most despise earthly happiness and who have particular control over the flesh, would place the supreme good in the base aspects of this life, as many through ignorance attribute to Epicurus and his followers, the Epicureans, surely not understanding what these meant by pleasure, as we just said. Otherwise, as we said, Seneca, that greatest upbuilder of morals, and himself of a most continent life, as you yourselves profess, would never have introduced the opinion of Epicurus for moral instruction so often as if he were his teacher, if, as is claimed, Epicurus had strayed from the path of sobriety and uprightness.

CHRISTIAN: It may be as you think, but answer this question: do those who understand pleasure in this way disagree in both terminology and meaning with those who use the name "virtue"?

---

[152] Augustine, *The City of God* 8.3, trs. G. G. Walsh and G. Monahan, p. 26.
[153] See Epicurus, "Letter to Menoeceus," tr. C. Bailey in W. J. Oates, ed., *The Stoic and Epicurean Philosophers* (New York, 1940), pp. 31-32.

PHILOSOPHER: In sum the distance between them is nothing or very small. In fact, to excel in the virtues is to have that peace of soul, and vice versa.

CHRISTIAN: Therefore, they both have the same opinion regarding the supreme good, but the terminology is different; and so what appeared to be two opinions regarding the supreme good are reduced to one.

PHILOSOPHER: I think so.

CHRISTIAN: And what, I ask, is the route they have established for arriving at this supreme good, that is virtue?

PHILOSOPHER: Surely the study of moral literature or exercise to gain control over the flesh, with the result that a good will strengthened into habit can be called virtue.

CHRISTIAN: And how do they define the notion of being blessed?

PHILOSOPHER: They say that to be blessed is to be well adapted, as it were, that is, to act in all things well and with ease; so that to be blessed is the same as to excel in good moral actions, that is, in the virtues.

CHRISTIAN: Do they not place a value on the immortality of the soul and on the beatitude of a future life, and expect the latter for their merits?

PHILOSOPHER: Yes, indeed, but what follows from this?

CHRISTIAN: Do they not judge the beatitude of that life to be greater where no painful suffering will afflict them when they have arrived, so that we should expect the supreme good of man and true beatitude there rather than here?

PHILOSOPHER: As you said, the greatest rest of that life is indeed free from all suffering. But when affliction ceases they say beatitude no longer increases unless virtue increases, and no one is said to become more blessed unless he becomes better in virtue. As I said, they identify being blessed with excellence in the virtues. Whence anyone, while he suffers for justice and is said to merit more by suffering, is said to be as blessed in torments as before because he is equally as good. For although his virtue now appears greater than before, yet it certainly does not increase because of the torment, but it is apparent from the torment how great the virtue was. If virtue keeps the mind fixed in the same intention, it would not be proper that anything which pertains to bodily rest or affliction should increase or diminish our beatitude. Finally, did your own Christ by suffering diminish his beatitude, or by rising increase it? Therefore, you should not think that we will be more blessed in that place because those bodily afflictions cease there, if we are not going to be better there.

CHRISTIAN: What if we are?

PHILOSOPHER: Then we will be more blessed because we are better.

CHRISTIAN: As I said, you expect that life for your merits as your due, as if the battle with vices were here and the crown of victory there.[154]

PHILOSOPHER: Yes, it is clear to all.

CHRISTIAN: So in what way is reward for suffering to be received there if living there is not happier, nor that life better and more blessed than the present? And if that life is more blessed than this one, then surely those who enjoy it are more blessed than they seem to be here.

PHILOSOPHER: Yes. As I said, more blessed if better; otherwise we do not receive it. For he who has received the crown is not for that reason endowed with greater virtue than he had before in the struggle, nor is his fortitude increased, although it is more proven and better known than before. In fact, the fatigue of the conflict could perhaps diminish it; and the life of the one who triumphs is not better than the life of the one who fights, although it is more pleasant.

CHRISTIAN: Your teachers as well as ours, and all men, count among evils: poverty, sickness, death, and the rest of the troubles which arise from adversity or from the passions. Because of these, which are the contraries of the virtues, there are many vices of the soul as well as of the body which, none-theless, are to be reckoned as evils, such as lameness of body or blindness, dullness of mind or forgetfulness.[155] In fact, when discussing contraries in his *Categories* Aristotle says:

---

[154] "Here, however, we strive by fighting, so that elsewhere as winners of the struggle we may receive a crown." Abelard, *Ethics*, ed. D. E. Luscombe, p. 13.

[155] Abelard, *Ethics*, ed. D. E. Luscombe, p. 3.

Indeed evil is necessarily the contrary of good and this is clearly shown by the induction of individual examples: as sickness is the contrary of health, injustice of justice, and weakness of strength. Likewise in other cases. But the contrary of evil is sometimes a good, sometimes an evil. For poverty, which is an evil, has excess for its contrary which is also an evil. But you will find this in only a few cases. In most cases, indeed, an evil is always the contrary of good.[156]

And in his *Topics* Tully, when he was assigning a topic by contraries, says, "If health is good then sickness is evil."[157] The Lord himself, speaking of the peace he grants to the obedient and of the persecution he sends against the rebellious, says through the Prophet, "I am the Lord; I make well-being and create woe."[158] With regard to earthly goods and evils, the Lord in the Gospel says to the rich man, "You received good things in your life-time, and Lazarus in like manner evil things."[159] Augustine, who was first one of yours and afterwards one of ours, also adds that death is an evil saying:

> For the simple reason that just as the law is not an evil though it increases the evil desires of sinners, so neither is death a good, though it increases the glory of sufferers and makes martyrs. And whereas the law is good because it is the prohibition of sin, death is evil because it is the wage of sin. Even as the unjust make evil use of good things, so the just make good use of evil

---

[156] Aristotle, *Categories* 13b35-14a5, in *Categoriae. Editio composita*, ed. by L. Minio-Paluello. Aristoteles latinus 1.1-5 (Paris, 1961), p. 74, l. 27 - p. 75, l. 3.

[157] Not in Cicero, but from Boethius, *De diff. top.* 3 (PL 64: 1198A) and used by Abelard, *Dialectica* 3, ed. L. M. De Rijk, 2nd ed., p. 441.

[158] Is 45, 6-7.

[159] Lk 16, 25.

things. And so it happens that evil men make evil use of the law although the law is a good thing and that good men die a good death although death is an evil thing.[160]

PHILOSOPHER: What do you have in view with these remarks, I pray?

CHRISTIAN: I say them that you may understand that that life is better which is clearly free from all those evils and is so utterly remote from sin that not only is there no sinning there but there is no possibility of sinning. That life was mistakenly proposed as a reward, unless it is better than the present or more pleasing. Moreover, if it is not more pleasing and better, it is irrationally preferred to this life; and those who desire it more act imprudently.

PHILOSOPHER: To speak the truth, I am certainly learning now that you are a first rate philosopher, and it is not right shamelessly to oppose such clear reasoning. But according to your proposed reasoning the supreme good of man must be expected there rather than here. And perhaps this was the view of Epicurus who says that pleasure is the supreme good since, after all, so great is the peace of soul that bodily affliction does not disturb it from without nor does any consciousness of sin disturb the mind from within, and vice does not hinder it, so that its perfect will is completely fulfilled. However, as long as something obstructs our will or is lacking, there is no true beatitude. But this surely is always the case while living here,

---

[160] Augustine, *The City of God* 13.5, trs. G. G. Walsh and G. Monahan, p. 306.

and the soul, burdened with the weight of an earthly body and as though enclosed in a prison, does not enjoy true liberty.

For who sometimes does not desire heat when it is too cold or vice versa, or fair weather when burdened with rain, or frequently more food or clothing than he has? There are also innumerable other things which, if we do not resist the evident truth, [we see] befall us when we do not want them or are denied us when we want them. And if we must judge that good of the future life to be the supreme good, as reason suggests, I think the route by which it is reached is the virtues by which we are adorned here. We will have to discuss these more carefully later.

CHRISTIAN: So you see, our disputation has led to this: we locate the supreme good of man or, as was said, the goal of the good, in the blessedness of a future life, and the route thereto in the virtues. But first I want to compare our, that is, the Christian teaching with regard to this supreme good, with yours so that whichever has the richer doctrine or exhortation concerning this good will be considered to be more perfect and will be more carefully attended to.

Moreover, in regard to the Old Law in which the Jews glory, you think you have successfully shown that this beatitude was not promised there as a reward, nor is any exhortation to it employed there. On the other hand, when the Lord Jesus was handing down the New Testament he established just such a foundation for his teaching right at the beginning where he encouraged contempt for the world and the desire for this beatitude as well, saying, "Blest are the poor in spirit, for theirs is the kingdom of heaven."[161] And further

[161] Mt 5, 3.

on: "Blest are those persecuted for justice' sake for theirs is the kingdom of heaven."[162] And if we give this careful attention [we see that] all his precepts or exhortations are employed to this end: that all prosperity is to be held in contempt or adversities tolerated out of hope for that highest and eternal life.

I do not think that your teachers have touched on this matter or invited your spirits to this goal of the good in a similar way. If they have, point it out by running through all the stipulations of your ethics. If you are unable to point it out, you should confess that the teaching of Christ is all the more perfect and better insofar as it exhorts us to the virtues for a better reason or hope, since you think that the virtues or their contraries ought to be desired or avoided for their own sake alone rather than for the sake of something else. Whence you think the former ought to be called uprightness and the latter lack of uprightness. In fact, you say that uprightness is what pleases through itself and is to be desired for itself, not for the sake of anything else;[163] just as, on the other hand, you say lack of uprightness is what is to be fled on account of its own proper baseness. For what is to be desired or avoided on account of something else you rather call useful or useless.

PHILOSOPHER: It surely did seem so to our forefathers as Tully sets down more fully in the second Book of his *Rhetoric*.[164] But surely when it is said: virtue is to be sought for its own sake

---

[162] Mt 5, 10.

[163] *Honestum* = "uprightness"; see Cicero, *De inventione* 2.52.157 and William of Conches, *Das Moralium dogma philosophorum des Guillaume de Conches lateinisch, altfranzösisch und mittelniederfränkisch* ed. J. Holmberg (Uppsala, 1929), p. 10.

[164] See Cicero, *De inventione* 2.52.157-158.

and not for the sake of something else.[165] reward for merits is not completely excluded, but reference to earthly benefits is removed. Otherwise we would not have properly established beatitude as the goal of the virtues, that is, the final cause, as your own Boethius says in the second Book of his *Topics*, following Themistius. There, when he gives an example of the topic of end, he says: "If to be blessed is good, then justice is good. For he says here: the goal of justice is such that if a person lives according to justice he is led to beatitude."[166] See, he clearly shows here that beatitude is given in recompense for a just life and we must have the intention of living justly in order to attain it.

In my view this beatitude is what Epicurus calls pleasure and what your Christ calls the kingdom of heaven. However, what does it matter by what name it is called as long as the reality remains the same and beatitude is not diverse, and the intention of living justly for the philosophers is not different from that of the Christians? For both you and we arrange to live here in justice in order to be glorified there; and we struggle here against vices in order to be crowned there with the merits for virtues, that is, we obtain that supreme good as the reward.

CHRISTIAN: But as far as I can see, our intention as well as our merits are considerably different from yours in this matter. And we are also not a little in disagreement concerning the supreme good itself.

---

[165] See Cicero, *De inventione* 2.54.164.
[166] Boethius, *De diff. top.* 2 (PL 64: 1189D).

PHILOSOPHER: I beg of you to clarify this if you can.

CHRISTIAN: It is incorrect to claim that something is the supreme good if something greater than it is found.[167] For what is less than or below something can in no way be called the supreme or the highest. But it is certain that every human beatitude or glory is greatly and ineffably surpassed by the divine. So no beatitude outside of the divine can properly be called the highest; or outside of it nothing is rightfully called the supreme good.

PHILOSOPHER: Here we do not mean the supreme good absolutely, but the supreme good of man.

CHRISTIAN: But we do not correctly say "the supreme good of man" when some greater good of man is found.

PHILOSOPHER: That is surely clear.

CHRISTIAN: So I ask whether one is more blessed than another in that beatitude, just as here on earth it happens that one is more just or holier than another, so that there is a diversity of reward corresponding to the diversity of merits.

PHILOSOPHER: What follows if that is the case?

---

[167] Reminiscent of Anselm's formula for God as "that than which none greater can be conceived." Anselm, *Proslogion* 1-4, tr. E. R. Fairweather, *A Scholastic Miscellany: Anselm to Ockham*, The Library of Christian Classics, 10 (Toronto, 1970). R. Thomas has drawn up a comparison between Abelard and Anselm in, *Der philosophisch-theologische Erkenntnisweg*, pp. 215-220.

CHRISTIAN: Indeed, because it is so you must concede that there one man becomes more blessed than another, and consequently the beatitude of the man which is less must not in any way be called the supreme good of man. So it is not proper that the man who is less blessed than another be now called blessed. Indeed, you have defined the supreme good as that which, when attained, makes one blessed. Therefore, either you should grant that the man who is less than another there has obtained the supreme good, or that he is in no way blessed, but only that person is blessed who has no one more blesssed than himself there. But if what is obtained makes him blessed then surely it is proper that it be called the supreme good according to the above definition.

PHILOSOPHER: Stop for a moment, I beg of you, and pay attention to what I will now say to this latest question. One is still allowed to correct what was poorly expressed since, as was said, we are conferring together in the search for truth and not in the display of cleverness.

CHRISTIAN: I grant and approve what you say. For it is not proper for us who are completely occupied in the search for truth to wrangle together after the manner of children or with rude shouting. And if something is conceded without due consideration, it is not proper for one who is intent on teaching or learning to take occasion from this to inflict embarrassment, where it should even be allowed to concede falsity sometimes for the sake of argument. So we grant complete freedom to change an opinion entirely or to correct it.

PHILOSOPHER: Please remember what I said and recall the conditional form where it was said, "What follows if that is the case?" For it seemed to many philosophers that all the virtues are present at the same time in all good men, and a person in whom some virtue is lacking is not to be considered good in any respect, and that for this reason there is no difference among good men either in the merits of this life or in the reward of beatitude. Now if this is perhaps correct, the same beatitude is rewarded to all, and all who have attained the same supreme good become equally blessed.

Tully clearly proposed this opinion in the second Book of the *De officiis* in these words:

> For even without the aid of prudence justice has considerable weight; but prudence without justice is of no avail to inspire confidence; for take from a man his reputation for probity, and the more shrewd and clever he is, the more hated and mistrusted he becomes. Therefore, justice combined with intelligence will command all the confidence we can desire; justice without prudence well be able to do much; prudence without justice will be of no avail at all. But I am afraid someone may wonder why I am now separating the virtues, as if it were possible for anyone to be just who is not at the same time prudent; for it is agreed upon among all philosophers, and I myself have often argued, that he who has one virtue has them all. There is one way of speaking when truth is being critically discussed, another when it is adapted to a general audience. And therefore, I am speaking here in the popular sense when I call some men brave, others good, others prudent; for when speaking in general we must employ familiar words in their common acceptation.[168]

---

[168] Cicero, *De officiis* 2.9.34-2.10.35. See Abelard, *Sic et Non*, "Prologue," eds. B. Polka and B. Zelechow, p. 108 and *Sic et Non* 137, eds. B. Boyer and R. McKeon, *Peter Abailard. Sic et Non. A Critical Edition* (Chicago, 1977), pp. 466-467 (PL 178: 1571c-D).

And in the *Paradoxes* he not only makes good men equal in virtues but even equates evil men in sins, so that he adds that all sins are equal.[169]

CHRISTIAN: Now for the first time I see that you have become shamelessly rash, wrangling rather than philosophizing. Indeed, fearing that you may seem to be compelled to confess what is clearly the truth, you turn to the insanity of the most obvious falsehood and are of the opinion that all good men are equally good and all guilty men are equally guilty, and all are deserving of the same glory or punishment as well.

PHILOSOPHER: If, indeed, it depends on the reality and not on the opinion of men who judge and reward the effect of actions more than the quality of morals, and who judge some more just or stronger or better or worse than others according to what appears to be done externally.

I certainly do not think that you are far from our opinion if you would carefully consider your teaching. In fact, as your own great philosopher, Augustine, affirms, charity includes all the virtues under one name and it alone, as he says, distinguishes between the sons of God and the sons of the devil.[170] And so he correctly says somewhere: "Where charity is, what can be lacking? Where it is absent, what can possibly be profit-

---

[169] Cicero, *Paradoxa stoicorum* 3.21, tr. H. Rackman, The Loeb Classical Library (Cambridge, Mass., 1942).

[170] Augustine, *Ten Homilies on the First Epistle of John* 5, tr. H. Browne revised by J. H. Myers, Nicene and Post-Nicene Fathers, First Series, 7 (New York, 1888), p. 491.

able"[171] "Indeed love is the fulfillment of the law."[172] The Apostle himself who says this, when he describes this fullness and excludes all evils from it while including all goods in it, says: "Love is patient, is kind. Love is not jealous, acts not perversely, etc."[173] Among other things, he says that it suffers all things or bears all things, even death. And as Christ reminds us, "There is no greater love than this: to lay down one's life for one's friends."[174] Therefore one person does not abound more in charity than another, since charity contains everything in itself and carries everything with itself. So if no one is superior to another in charity, he is certainly not so in virtues or merits since charity includes every virtue, as you say.

CHRISTIAN: Indeed, if virtue is understood in the proper sense as that which obtains merit with God, charity alone must be called virtue. But if it is understood as that which makes a person just or strong or temperate, it is properly called justice or fortitude or temperance. But just as all who have charity are not equally inflamed by it, nor do all prudent people have equal understanding, so all just persons are not equally just or all equally strong or temperate. And although we grant that all the virtues are in some people according to the distinction of species, when for instance one of them is just and strong and temperate, nonetheless, we do not grant that they are equal in virtues or merits, since it happens that one individual is more just or stronger or more modest than another. For although we

---

[171] Augustine, *Lectures on the Gospel according to St. John* 83, trs. J. Gibb and J. Innes, Nicene and Post-Nicene Fathers, First Series, 7 (New York, 1888), p. 349.

[172] Rom 13, 10.

[173] 1 Cor 13, 4.

[174] Jn 15, 13.

acknowledge that individuals share in the above mentioned species of the virtues, there is, nonetheless, a great difference in the individuals of the species since one man's justice or fortitude or temperance may be greater than another's. And so although charity confers all that you said, it does not grant all to each individual in whom it exists. For just as everything appropriate to the body is provided by nature, but not everything to all, likewise in the goods of the soul or the virtues it happens that all are not equally enriched by all the virtues.

Whence I want you to notice how weak that argument is, yes a vile sophism which the aforesaid philosopher, from the opinion of others, represents in a paradox to demonstrate that the virtues as well as the vices are equal in everyone when he said that "No one is better than a good man, no one more temperate than a temperate man, no one braver than a brave man, nor anyone wiser than a wise man."[175]

Though someone may not be better than a good man, however, he is better than some particular good man. For what is it to say of someone that he is better than a good man except that he is better than any good man whatsoever? When we say that God is better than man we mean nothing else than that he surpasses all men. Likewise, when we say that some good man is better than a good man, that is, better than a good man is good, or better than some good man is good, it seems that this must be understood in no other way than that in general he is set above all good men. But this is completely false since he himself is also one of the good men. For if he is better than a good man or better than some good man is good, it seems to follow that neither a good man nor some good man is as good;

---

[175] Cicero, *Paradoxa stoicorum* 3.21.

but if someone is good then he is less good than he. So it seems to be very important whether someone is said to be better than some good man or better than some good man is good. And here indeed the snare of sophism can occur in every comparison; just as they try to show that all good men are equally good, they likewise try to show that any handsome men whatsoever are equally handsome since clearly no handsome man is more handsome than a handsome man simply and in general, but he may be more handsome than another handsome man.

Who, finally, does not understand that it is the height of insanity to say that all sins are equal? For whether you locate sin in the will or in action, it is clear that among evil men one has a more evil will than another and acts in a more harmful or worse way. The will of course leads to action, and when the opportunity for harming is present one person does more harm than another or persecutes some just person more because he hates him more and desires to inflict more torment. Similarly, all good people do not equally do good or wish to do so. From this it is clear that good men are not equal to one another nor are evil men; nor should their merits be equated so that the reward is also understood to be equal.

Furthermore, with the opinion of the foolish put aside, if you would consider the excellent teaching of proven philosophers concerning the virtues, and attend to the careful fourfold distinction of the virtues provided by Plotinus, the most learned of men, that is, the distinction into: political virtues, purifying virtues, virtues of the purified mind, exemplary virtues,[176] from their names and descriptions you

---

[176] See Macrobius, *Commentary on the Dream of Scipio* 1.8, translated

are bound to admit at once that men differ greatly in virtue. The Apostle whom you used against us did not overlook this difference when he spoke of continence and of the permission to marry. He says: "I would that all men were as I am. Still, each one has his own gift from God, one this and another that."[177] Distinguishing the rewards of the future life according to the quality of virtues or merits he says: "Star differs from star in brightness. So it will be with the resurrection of the dead."[178] And in another place, "He who sows sparingly will also reap sparingly."[179]

While he did say that charity is the fullness of the Law, that is, the Law is fulfilled through charity, this does not prove that all are equal in charity, since charity extends beyond command. And there is that exhortation of Truth who says: "When you have done all you have been commanded to do, say: We are useless servants. We have done what it was our duty to do."[180] In other words, you should count it as very little if you accomplish only what you are obliged to by precept unless, that is, you add a gratuitous dimension to the obligation of precept. And the expression, "We have done what it was our duty to do," is another way of saying: in discharging precepts we fulfill our duties and perform necessary actions, as it were, not gratuitous actions. But when someone rises to the eminence of virginity he surely transcends the order of precept since he is not obliged to it by precept. The Apostle says the

with an introduction and notes. W. H. Stahl, Records of Civilization: Sources and Studies, 48 (New York, 1952), p. 121.

[177] 1 Cor 7, 7. See Abelard, *Ethics*, ed. D. E. Luscombe, p. 23.

[178] 1 Cor 15, 41-42.

[179] 2 Cor 9, 6.

[180] Lk 17, 10.

same: "Now, with respect to virgins, I have not received any commandment from the Lord, but I give my opinion."[181] Even in those who have fulfilled the Law but do not go beyond it charity can be unequal since, evidently, in the same action the fervor of charity may be greater in one than in another.

Concerning the objection taken from Augustine's words, "Where charity is, what can be lacking, etc.," there is no one who thinks that he took this in such a way as to be willing to join all men together in the virtues and in merits. He who is a follower of both the Lord and the Apostle contradicts this interpretation almost everywhere. Surely what he means is this: what could be lacking for salvation, but not for the perfection of virtue? To be sure, no one who has it perishes, but all are not equal in it.

PHILOSOPHER: I pray that you not be troubled by our introduction of many views or opinions in our attempt to elicit the rational truth from each of them. For those who look for a place hitherto unknown are forced to explore many paths in order to be able to choose the more correct one, just as I am compelled to do now in inquiring into the supreme good when I propose the views of our forefathers or my own personal views on your request.

CHRISTIAN: It would not be troublesome if what is introduced as opinion, though not true, were to have at least some degree of probability. For there is no need to refute with reason what is manifestly false.

---

[181] 1 Cor 7, 25.

PHILOSOPHER: What if we were to say that the supreme good of man is that state of a future life in comparison only with the goods of the present life? For although you say that God proposed two ends to us, the supreme good in heaven or the supreme evil in hell, you understand these only in relation to the good or evil state of the present life. In fact, reason suggests to us six states of man, three in this life and in parallel with these another three in the future. The first state of man is surely the state into which he is born while he has not yet acquired freedom of choice through an awakened reason which allows him to be called a good man or a bad man according to his choices, although he himself is a good thing or a good substance or a good creature. Once he has become a good or bad man he has indeed entered into the good or evil state of man from the prior state of man since, after reaching the age of discretion, he has knowingly inclined to good or to evil. Indeed, the first state of man is properly said to be like an indifferent state, neither good nor evil; the second is good if it ascends to the virtues, if it descends to the vices it is evil.

Likewise, the future life has three states. One is like the indifferent state, properly speaking neither blessed nor wretched. This is the state of those whose state was also indifferent in this life, as we described, bereft of all virtues and merits, when human reason is not yet awakened. The others are: the best state for merits, and the worst state. Moreover, I think these latter two are to be called the supreme good and the supreme evil in comparison with the other two of the present life which merit them because nothing adverse or beneficial is mixed with them. And it is clear that the other two have such a mixture, so that neither good nor evil are in them in a pure form.

CHRISTIAN: So according to you, the rest of the celestial life must be understood to be the supreme good, just as, on the other hand, the future damnation of evil men must be understood to be the supreme evil. We obtain both through our merits, as you mentioned; and it is through these, as though by certain paths, that we arrive there.

PHILOSOPHER: Yes, that is my view and it is clear. In fact, no view is held more firmly by those who embrace the natural law than that virtue suffices for beatitude, and because the virtues alone make us blessed, no other path can claim this name. So, on the other hand, it is evident that a truly wretched state comes about only through vices. Consequently, it is evident that just as the former are the paths to the supreme good, so the latter are the paths to the supreme evil.

CHRISTIAN: Since you now seem to have made some progress towards the supreme good of man and towards his supreme evil, and moreover, you have touched on the paths leading to them, you can relax the reins of your objections somewhat on your course so that you might more easily reach your proposed goal and be able to judge the completion of the task more truly and more perfectly. Having shown what you call the supreme good of man or his supreme evil, it remains for you also to define carefully and to distinguish what you have called their paths, that is, the virtues and vices, so that they may be more desired or avoided the better they are known.[182]

---

[182] See Abelard, *Dialectica* 4, ed. L. M. De Rijk, 2nd ed., p. 469, where Abelard remarks on the necessity of knowing evil before it can be avoided.

PHILOSOPHER: "Virtue," they say "is an excellent habit of the mind,"[183] just as, on the other hand, I think vice is the worst habit of the mind. Indeed we call "habit" what Aristotle distinguished in the *Categories* when he locates the first species of quality in habit and disposition.[184] For habit is a quality of a thing not present in it by nature but acquired by striving and deliberation, and which is difficult to alter. So the chastity which they call natural in some people, resulting from frigidity of the body or from some constitution of nature,[185] which does not have to struggle against concupiscence over which it might triumph and which does not obtain merit, we in no wise reckon among the virtues. The same is true of any qualities of mind which are easily altered. Indeed, where there is no fight against opposition there is no crown for a conquering virtue, even according to the statement of your great philosopher: "He is not crowned unless he has competed according to the rules."[186] And Philosophy says to Boethius in the fourth Book of the *Consolation*, "For which cause virtue is so called because

---

[183] The definition is from Boethius, *De divisione* (PL 64: 885B) and is used as an example of conversion of terms, not in an ethical discussion, and is mentioned by Abelard, *Sic et Non* 144, eds. Boyer and McKeon, p. 497 (PL 178: 1591B). This definition is used by Abelard and his school side by side with another: "Virtue is a habit of the well constituted mind." See Abelard, *Ethics*, ed. D. E. Luscombe, p. 129, and Hermannus, *Epitomae theologiae* 32 (PL 178: 1749D). The latter definition seems also to have its source in Boethius, *De diff. top.* 2 (PL 64: 1188C). For Hermannus see D. E. Luscombe, *The School of Peter Abelard. The Influence of Abelard's Thought on the Early Scholastic Period*, Cambridge Studies in Medieval Life and Thought, N.S., 14 (Cambridge, 1969), pp. 158-164.

[184] Aristotle, *Categories* 8b25, in *Categoriae. Editio composita*, ed. by L. Minio-Paluello, p. 63; see Abelard, *Ethics*, ed. D. E. Luscombe, p. 129.

[185] See Abelard, *Ethics*, ed. D. E. Luscombe, p. 5.

[186] 2 Tm 2, 5.

it has sufficient strength to overcome adversity."[187] Again, he asserts that every virtue is difficult to alter when, in the above mentioned tract on quality, he comments on Aristotle who places the sciences and the virtues among the habits. He says: "Unless it is difficult to alter it is not virtue. Nor is one just who judges justly on one occasion, nor is he an adulterer who commits adultery once, but only when this will and frame of mind are stable."[188]

In truth, it is that excellent habit of mind which molds us for the merit of true beatitude; and such are the individual species of virtue which some determine to be many, some fewer. Indeed, Socrates,[189] through whom the study of moral discipline first or principally gained strength, distinguished four species of virtue: prudence, justice, fortitude, temperance.

But some say that the discretion of prudence is the mother or source of the virtues rather than a virtue itself.[190] Prudence is surely the very knowledge of morals which, as a treatise on ethics teaches, is the knowledge of good and evil things,[191]

[187] Boethius, *Consolation of Philosophy* 4, prose 7, in *The Theological Tractates. The Consolation of Philosophy*, trs. H. F. Stewart and E. K. Rand, The Loeb Classical Library (Cambridge, Mass., 1962), p. 359.

[188] Boethius, *In Categorias* 3 (PL 64: 242B); see Abelard, *Sic et Non* 144, eds. Boyer and McKeon, p. 497 (PL 178: 1590-1591).

[189] For Abelard's probable source here, see Augustine, *The City of God* 8.3, trs. G. G. Walsh and G. Monahan, p. 24; or Isidore, *Isidori Hispalensis episcopi Etymologiarum sive originum libri XX*, ed. W. M. Lindsay (Oxford, 1911), 2.24.

[190] See *Johannes Cassiani Conlationes XXIIII*, 2.4, ed. M. Petschenig, Corpus scriptorum ecclesiasticorum latinorum 13: 44; *De vitis patrum* 4.42 (PL 73: 840D-841A); St. Bernard, *Sermones super Cantica canticorum* 49, S. Bernardi opera 2, eds. J. Leclercq et al. (Rome, 1958), 76. See Abelard: "For discretion is the mother of all the virtues," Sermon 30 (PL 178: 567D), and *Ethics*, ed. D. E. Luscombe, p. 129.

[191] Cicero, *De inventione* 2.53.160.

which indeed are properly to be called goods or evils in themselves. For certain things are of themselves and as it were substantially called good or evil, such as the virtues or the vices. Others are so accidentally and through something else; for example, our actions, although they are indifferent in themselves, nevertheless are said to be good or evil on account of the intention from which they proceed.[192] Consequently, when the same thing is done by different people or by the same person at different times, the same action is, nevertheless, often said to be good and evil because of the difference of intentions. What are called good or evil substantially and of their own nature, however, remain always in such an unmixed state that what is once good can never become evil, or vice versa. And so the discernment both of these goods and of these evils is called prudence.

Indeed, because this discretion can be in good men as well as in evil men and does not have merit, it is never correctly called virtue or an excellent habit of the mind. So Aristotle, distinguishing the sciences from the virtues and giving examples of habit in the above mentioned treatise on quality, says, "Such are the sciences or the virtues."[193] Boethius, in commenting on this passage, says, "For Aristotle, unlike Socrates, does not consider the virtues to be knowledge."[194] Likewise, as I already mentioned above, Augustine, first one of ours and afterwards one of yours, sometimes extends the term "virtue" even to faith and hope, sometimes he restricts it to charity alone which

[192] For Abelard on indifferent acts see, *Ethics*, ed. D. E. Luscombe, p. 45, p. 46 n. 1, and p. 47.

[193] Aristotle, *Categories* 8b30, in *Categoriae. Editio composita*, ed. by L. Minio-Paluello, p. 63; see Abelard, *Ethics*, ed. D. E. Luscombe, p. 129.

[194] Boethius, *In Categorias* 3 (PL. 64: 242c).

surely pertains properly and especially to good men, since the
other two are common to the reprobate as well as to the elect.
In fact, it is written. "Faith without works is useless,"[195] and,
"The expectation of the wicked comes to nought."[196] However,
just as faith or hope without works become useless or rather
harmful for us, so also prudence. For we are more guilty either
when we knowingly avoid what we ought to do, or when we
do what must not be done, than if this were to happen through
ignorance which would be able to offer some excuse. You
know it is written: "The slave who knew his master's wishes
but did not prepare to fulfill them will get a severe beating."[197]
And elsewhere: "It were better not to have known the way of
truth, than having known it, to turn back."[198] So prudence as
well as faith or hope, which are common to evil men as well as
to good men, are not to be called virtues as much as they are to
be said to offer a certain guidance or inducement to the virtues.

CHRISTIAN: I think this is enough for the present concerning
prudence. Now it remains for you to pass on to the rest of the
virtues which were distinguished by Socrates.

PHILOSOPHER: Justice is the virtue which gives every man his
due while preserving the common advantage.[199] It is the virtue
by which we will that each and every one have what he
deserves as long as it causes no common harm. For it often
happens that while we give to someone his due in accordance

[195] Jas 2, 17.
[196] Prv 10, 28.
[197] Lk 12, 47.
[198] 2 Pt 2, 21.
[199] Cicero, *De inventione* 2.53.160.

with his merits, this act towards an individual causes common harm. Therefore, lest the part be prejudicial to the whole and the individual to the community, the phrase "preserving the common advantage" is added. In fact it is proper that everything we do be correctly referred to this end, namely, that in all things a person attend not so much to his own good as to the common good, that he care more for the public interest than for domestic matters, and that he live more for his country than for himself.

Consequently, that first and greatest teacher of moral philosophy, Socrates, was of the opinion that everything was to be held in common and to be applied to the common advantage. To this end he established that wives were also to be held in common so that no one would recognize his own children. That is, one should not believe that children are begotten for oneself but rather for the country, so that this community of wives is clearly not to be understood in reference to carnal pleasure but in reference to the fruit of offspring.[200]

Aulus Fulvius left an example of this to the memory of posterity in word as well as in deed by killing his own son, saying that "He had begotten him not for Catilina against his country but for his country against Catilina."[201] Burning with

---

[200] For Abelard's source here, see Plato, *Timaeus* 18c-d, in *Timaeus a Calcidio translatus commentarioque instructus*, ed. J. H. Waszink, Corpus Platonicorum medii aevi, Plato latinus 4 (London, 1962), p. 9; Abelard, *Theol. christ.* 2.46-48, CC.CM 12: 150-151.

[201] Valerius Maximus, *Factorum et dictorum memorabilium libri novem* 5.5, ed. C. Kempf, 2nd ed., Bibliotheca scriptorum Graecorum et Romanorum Teubneriana. Scriptores Romani (Leipzig, 1888); Abelard, *Theol. christ.* 2.48, CC.CM 12: 151.

zeal for justice and seeing in the son not his son but an enemy of the country, he demonstrated the aforesaid definition of justice not so much with his mouth as with his hand.

Consequently, whoever is steadfast in this will which we have spoken of so that he cannot be easily moved from it is accomplished in the virtue of justice even if he has not yet been perfected in fortitude and temperance. But because what is lost with difficulty is nonetheless sometimes compelled to recede for some great intervening cause, just as this good will which is called justice sometimes dies away because of fear or cupidity, fortitude is necessary against fear, and temperance against cupidity. Indeed, if the fear of something which we do not will or the lustful desire for what we do will are so great as to prevail over reason, they easily turn the mind from its good intention and lead to the contraries. Therefore, fortitude takes up the shield against fear, and temperance the bridle against lustful desire so that, strengthened by these virtues, we are able to carry out in deed, as far as in us lies, what we already will through the virtue of justice. So we call both of these a certain firmness and constancy of mind by which we are rendered able to carry out what we will through justice. And indeed their contraries are correctly called certain infirmities of mind and incapacities in resisting vices, such as laziness and pusillanimity which make man negligent, and intemperance which releases us to obscene pleasures or to base desires.

Fortitude is the considered, that is, reasonable endurance of trials and the undertaking of dangerous tasks.[202] This is the virtue which makes us ready to undertake dangers or to endure hardships when the situation calls for it, and it particularly

---

[202] Cicero, *De inventione* 2.54.163.

depends on the love of justice which we call good zeal in repelling or avenging evils.

Temperance is a firm and moderate control exercised by reason over lust and other improper impulses of the mind.[203] For often, while seeming to ourselves temperate, we overstep the limit and transgress the bounds of temperance with the result that while we are zealous for sobriety we afflict ourselves with immoderate fasts, and while we desire to conquer vice we extinguish nature itself. In this way, through many excesses we establish vices which resemble virtues in place of the virtues themselves. So it is fitting that the term "moderate" was added after the term "firm."

And surely it is necessary that over this reason the reason of prudence rule which, as we said, they call the mother of the virtues, that is, their source and nurse. For unless we become acquainted with the virtues beforehand through it and are able to distinguish them carefully not only from their contrary and manifest vices but also from vices appearing as virtues, we do not give our attention to gaining or retaining them since we have no knowledge of them. So, whoever is accomplished in these virtues must of necessity have prudence. It is through it, surely, that justice, which dispenses merits, comes to know what is owed to whom, fortitude possesses discretion in undertaking dangers or withstanding trials, and temperance, as was said, possesses moderation in curbing concupiscence. So it is clear that in these three virtues which we mentioned and from which prudence cannot be lacking, man is accomplished and perfected in the good. Now it remains to distinguish their species or parts so that we might recognize them more

[203] Cicero, *De inventione* 2.54.164.

carefully and more truly judge the teaching concerning them by running through each individually.[204]

CHRISTIAN: Yes, we desire that this be done since it is agreeable and ought to be agreeable.

PHILOSOPHER: If I may speak briefly, the following pertain to justice which consists in conserving for each what is his: reverence, beneficence, veracity, and vindication.

What is reverence?

We say reverence is that part of justice whereby we are willing to show due veneration to all: to God, which is called religion, as well as to men who are deserving because of power or some merit, which is called respect. And it is clear that the virtue of obedience is included here through which we also show honor to superiors by submitting to their commands because we in no way hold their reasonable regulations in contempt.

What is beneficence?

Beneficence is surely that by which we are disposed to offer due assistance to the distress of men either by granting necessities to those in need, for instance, which is called generosity (since prodigality consists in giving luxuries), or by liberating those who are violently oppressed, which is called clemency.

---

[204] The following divisions are grounded on Macrobius, *Commentary on the Dream of Scipio* 1.8 and paralleled in Abelard's contemporaries, but the actual divisions are original with Abelard. For a comparative study of similar divisions contemporary with or shortly after Abelard see, R. Baron, "A propos des ramifications des vertus au XIIᵉ siècle," *Recherches de théologie ancienne et médiévale* 23 (1956) 19-39.

Our forefathers called mercy, which comes from the word "miseries," a vice and a certain infirmity of soul rather than a virtue. Through it we desire to come to the aid of others out of a natural compassion simply because they are afflicted. But clemency is moved to come to the aid of some only out of reasonable affection and it attends not so much to the fact that they are afflicted as to the fact that they are unjustly afflicted, so that by avoiding injustice it complies with justice. Moreover, they are not acts of justice when we come to the aid of others unless in this we render to them their due. But since virtue is a habit of the mind which is surely acquired more through application or endeavor than by nature, as is clear from the above, such natural compassion must not be numbered among the virtues. Through it we are concerned with coming to the aid even of criminals themselves who are in affliction, out of a certain human or carnal affection, not out of a reasonable affection. But in this we are rather the adversaries of justice, hindering the application of due punishment to them. Finally, whatever may happen, to submit the mind to sorrow is proper to infirmity rather than to virtue, to misery rather than to beatitude, and to confusion of mind not to peace of mind. For since nothing is done without a cause because God disposes all things in the best manner, on what grounds should the just man sorrow or be sad, and so go against the perfect disposition of God to the best of his power, as if he thought it needed correction?

What is veracity?

Veracity is that by which we strive to keep our promises to those to whom we are so bound. For if we promise what we ought not we are not guilty by not fulfilling it, since a bad promise does not put us in anyone's debt. For he who carries out what should not have been promised doubles the effect of an evil deed when he adds a perverse deed to a perverse promise and does not choose to correct the bad promise by suspending the deed.

What is vindication?

Vindication is the steadfast desire of taking vengeance by which due punishment is inflicted for faults which have been committed.

However, it is certain that the phrase "preserving the common advantage" which we previously placed in the definition of justice, is to be understood in the definition of each of the four parts of justice. For, as we also recalled above, the proper goal of our actions is that each seek not so much his own but the common advantage and live not so much for himself as for all men, according to the statement of Lucanus which he proclaimed in praise of Cato: "For he alone, free from love and free from hate, had leisure to wear mourning for mankind."[205] Again: "Such was the character, such the inflexible rule of austere Cato, to observe moderation and hold fast to the limit, to follow nature, to give his life for his country, to believe that he was born to serve the whole world and not himself."[206] And after a few lines: "For the state he became a father and a husband, good for all the people."[207]

Indeed, the person who attends to his own interests is of a weak nature, and the one who attends to the interests of others is possessed of superior virtue. The person who cares only for

[205] Lucan, *Pharsalia* 2, lines 377-378, tr. J. D. Duff, *The Civil War*, The Loeb Classical Library (Cambridge, Mass., 1928).

[206] Lucan, *Pharsalia* 2, lines 380-383.

[207] Lucan, *Pharsalia* 2, lines 388-390.

himself and is satisfied with his own interests ought to think little of his own life and does not merit the gratitude and praise of others. Each ought in his own small way to imitate God who, since he has no need of anything, takes no care for himself but cares for all, and ministers not to his own needs but to the needs of all. He is the governor of the whole fabric of the world as of one great republic.

There are those who distinguish the parts of justice into a greater number, not of real parts but of names, and divide into many what we have comprised under one word. What is included in the whole they divide into parts, for example: piety towards parents; and friendship, that is, good will towards those who love us for their sake more than for the hope of some advantage, with a similar will on their part towards us; and gratitude in recompense for benefits. But surely it is clear that these three are placed under beneficence by which the mind is ready to render any benefits due to parents as well as to others.

Of Natural or Positive Justice

However, in matters of justice one must not only not stray from the path of natural justice, but one must also not stray from the path of positive justice. Indeed, one right is called natural, another positive. Natural right is what reason, which is naturally in everyone and so remains permanent in all, moves us to perform, such as to worship God, to love parents, to punish evildoers,[208] and the observance of these is so necessary for all that without them no merits suffice.[209]

---

[208] See Cicero, *De inventione* 2.53.161.
[209] In his *Problemata Heloissae* 15 (PL. 178: 703A-B) Abelard distinguishes

The right of positive justice is what is instituted by men to safeguard utility or uprightness more securely or to extend them, and is based on custom alone or on written authority, for example, the punishments of vengeance or the sentences of judges in the examination of accusations. For with some people there is the custom of duels or of hot iron, but with others the oath is the end of every controversy and every discussion is committed to witnesses. So when we must live with others we must also hold to their institutions which we mentioned, just as we hold to natural rights.

The Laws which you call divine, namely the Old and New Testaments, also lay down certain natural precepts which you call moral, such as the precept to love God or neighbor, not to commit adultery, not to steal, not to murder. But some have the nature of positive justice which were suited to some peoples at a certain time, such as circumcision for the Jews and baptism for you, and several others whose precepts you call figurative.[210] The Roman pontiffs or synods also enact new decrees every day or grant dispensations by which you say what was previously lawful becomes unlawful or vice versa, as

---

between moral precepts of the Law and figurative precepts. The moral precepts seem to be precepts of the natural law which are naturally in all "and had to be carried out by everyone, and were given prior to a written law and necessarily make up men's moral complement, so that unless what they command is carried out no one merited salvation. Such are: to love God and neighbor, not to kill, not to fornicate or lie, and the like, and unless they are followed no one can be justified."

[210] "Figurative precepts of the Law, in their literal interpretation, confer no justice by being carried out, but were instituted temporarily to prefigure something pertaining to justice, such as the observance of the Sabbath, circumcision, abstinence from certain foods, and the like." Abelard, *Problemata Heloissae* 15 (PL. 178: 703B).

if God had placed in their power by their precepts or permissions to make good or evil what were not so before, and as if their authority could pass judgment on our law.

However, it now remains to turn the pen to the other two species of virtue after the consideration of justice.

Of the Parts of Fortitude

Fortitude seems to us to be comprised of two parts: magnanimity and endurance.

What is Magnanimity?

Magnanimity is that by which we are prepared to take on the most arduous tasks when there is a reasonable cause.

What is Endurance?

Endurance is that by which we steadfastly persevere in carrying out this resolution.

Of the Parts of Temperance

It seems to me, and I don't think you disagree, that these are the parts of temperance: humility, frugality, meekness, chastity, sobriety.

What is Humility?

Humility is that whereby we so temper our desire for vain glory that we have no desire to appear higher than we really are.

What is Frugality?

Frugality is the bridle on excess by which, for instance, we spurn the possession of that which is beyond what is necessary. Likewise, meekness is the bridle on anger, chastity on lust, and sobriety on gluttony.

And it should be noted that, since justice is the steadfast will of the mind which preserves for each what is his, fortitude and temperance are certain powers and the strength of the mind by which, as we recalled above, the good will of justice is fortified. Since their contraries consist in a lack of power, it is surely clear that they are powers. Indeed, weakness of the mind, which is contrary to fortitude, is its sickness and impotence which we can call laziness or pusillanimity. Intemperance is also opposed to temperance and is a certain weakness and impotence of the mind which renders it incapable of resisting those of its impulses which are contrary to reason. Through these the infirm mind is drawn into the miserable captivity of vice as if by military attendants, and it becomes a slave-girl of what it ought to master. And just as justice is that good will we mentioned, so injustice is the contrary will. Justice indeed makes man good, while fortitude and temperance make him able, since they enable us to carry out what we will through justice.

However, I believe that in the above discussion I have distinguished the species or parts of virtue in such a way that all the steps are included in them by which beatitude is reached and the supreme good is obtained for merits. Now we are prepared to listen if you, in your prudence, decide to approve or to reject something of the above, or if, perhaps, you think something must be added to complete these remarks.

CHRISTIAN: Yes, this is surely agreeable. But before we come to these steps to the supreme good which you have proposed, let us return to the debate about the supreme good and the supreme evil which was interrupted but not abandoned. We should determine what the supreme good or the supreme evil are to be called in an absolute sense, and whether the supreme good is other than the supreme good of man, or whether the supreme evil is other than the supreme evil of man.

Return to the inquiry concerning the supreme good which had been interrupted.

PHILOSOPHER: Certainly it is clear that with all those who philosophize correctly the supreme good is said and believed to be none other than God whose incomparable and ineffable beatitude knows no beginning or end and which can be neither increased nor diminished. And I believe that the supreme evil is the supreme misery or the cruelest punishment of anything, whether of man or of any other creature. However, I understand man's supreme good or his supreme evil to be the rest of a future life or perpetual punishment, as I already recalled and established above. So, as to the question of the relationship between the supreme good in itself and the supreme good of man, I think the answer is, as is clear from the foregoing, that the supreme good is God himself or the supreme tranquility of his beatitude which we judge to be none other than God himself who is blessed of himself and not through another. However, the supreme good of man is that perpetual rest or joy which everyone receives for his merits after this life, whether it occurs in the very vision or knowledge of God, as you say, or in some other way. The supreme evil is the supreme misery or punishment of any creature which is received for its merits, as I said. However, we call the supreme evil of man those torments of men received in the hereafter in recompense for their merits.

Of the Supreme Evil

CHRISTIAN: As far as I can see, you understand the supreme evil itself as well as the supreme evil of man to be only the punishments in the future world which are rendered in recompense for merits.

PHILOSOPHER: Yes, certainly.

CHRISTIAN: But surely those punishments which are applied in recompense for merits are also just, since it is just to punish in this way those who deserved it. But it is well known that whatever is just is good. So those punishments which you call the supreme evil or the supreme evil of man are undoubtedly good. Consider therefore whether you don't appear to grant that what is good rather than what is evil is the supreme evil. For I do not see what reason you have to call the supreme evil or the supreme evil of man what is in no wise evil.

PHILOSOPHER: You ought to remember what you yourself pointed out above, using our authorities as well as your own, namely, that every affliction is also an evil rather than a good. But I do not think that one must therefore conclude that every affliction is evil. In fact, it is often the case that a change in the gender of adjectives varies the meaning, so that it is one thing to say that punishment is good and another to say that punishment is a good, that is, a good thing. Likewise, it is one thing to say that this bronze statue is everlasting, which is false; another to say it is an everlasting thing, that is, something which is everlasting, which is true in the sense that bronze itself is a lasting and durable nature. And although every proposition is something composite, nevertheless, not every proposition is a composite proposition, but only the one which has propositions as parts, that is, the hypothetical. And we do not say that every phrase, which we know to be a composite thing, is composite, nor do we grant that every phrase which we call simple is a simple thing. Likewise, when we say that some punishment is just or good because surely it is just or good that the person who is punished be afflicted in this way, nonetheless, we are not for that reason compelled to grant that it is a just or good thing.

And although you say that every creature is good because all of God's creation is good,[211] and you do not deny that this man who is evil is also a creature and for this reason you claim that he who is evil is a good thing, still you do not admit that he is thereby a good man. Surely no man must be said to be good except the one who is adorned with good morals; but even what is lacking in reason and inanimate can be called a good thing or a good creature. And although God is said to have created all things good, and this very small man or this horse were already created by him, although they were created good things, nonetheless, they were not already created a good man or a good horse. Nor did God create either a good man or an evil man when he created this very small man who will become evil; but he fashioned him as a good thing or the substance of a good nature. And the horse which will never be a good horse, he did not create as a good horse, although he might seem to create some horses vicious, namely those which are said to contract some viciousness in their very creation and consequently are afterwards useless or of very little use. It is also clear that men themselves naturally contract some vices because of the arrangement of the elements in their creation so

[211] See Boethius, *De hebdomadibus*, trs. H. F. Stewart and E. K. Rand, *The Theological Tractates*, The Loeb Classical Library (Cambridge, Mass., 1962).

that, for example, they become naturally angry or lustful or troubled with other vices.

And in regard to that angel who, as 'bearer of light' (Lucifer), was preferred to the others and who, as you say, later apostasized, perhaps God did not create him as a good angel or a good spirit since, as you say, he did not remain in the truth or in the love of God. Many of your own claim that charity once had is never lost.[212] Indeed no angel or rational spirit or even man who is alienated from the love of God and true charity is rightfully called good, just as he is not called evil as long as he is wanting in sin. If, therefore, that angel was not created with sin or the love of God, how is one to say that he was at that time created a bad or a good angel?

It is the same for individual men. When they are created without the use of reason, they must not be called either good men or bad men at the time of creation, since they do not receive the quality of being either good men or bad men through their creation. But since some of them are naturally feeble or even stupid, and they are born filled with different afflictions of soul as well as of body, and all men are created mortal, clearly, the good substance of human nature shares in many evils from its very creation. For as Aristotle reminds us and clear truth attests, the contrary of good can only be an evil.[213] So it is clear that mortality as well as the rest of the afflictions we have just mentioned and with which we are born must be numbered among evils, since no one doubts that their

[212] See Abelard, *Sic et Non* 138, eds. Boyer and McKeon, pp. 470-484 (PL 178: 1574-1582).

[213] Aristotle, *Categories* 13b35-14a5, in *Categoriae. Editio composita*, ed. by L. Minio-Paluello, p. 74.

contraries are goods; and some vices or evils are naturally in some good substances from creation itself, such as mortality in man and lack of reason in the horse. For although mortality is not called a vice of man since, clearly, no one is worse than another on the basis of it in which all share equally, however, it is a certain vice of nature in man himself, since human nature in this is worse or more infirm than a nature which is immortal.

Therefore, just as we grant that any man, sullied by no matter what vices, is a good thing, but we do not grant that he is a good man for that reason, so, on the other hand, we say that any punishment is an evil thing, although we say that some punishment is good. So you see, it does not follow that if we establish that good and just punishment is the supreme evil of man, that we grant that his supreme evil is a good thing for that reason. And although that punishment is good, as was said, it must not for that reason be said to be simply good, that is, a good thing.

CHRISTIAN: Let us grant for now, as you say, that on the basis of your previous claims you surely cannot be accused of holding that the supreme evil of man is a good thing, although you do not deny that the punishment which is good and just is the supreme evil. But again I ask: since the fault preceding the punishment as well as the resulting punishment are evils, which of them must be said to be the worse and greater evil of man – the fault which makes man evil, or the punishment which God inflicts in executing a just judgment on him?

PHILOSOPHER: I think that a man's fault is certainly a worse evil than its punishment. Since there is no doubt that among evils the greater evil is what displeases God more and is worthy of punishment, who would doubt that the fault is worse than punishment for the fault? It is surely because of his fault that a man displeases God and is consequently called evil, not because of the punishment which is inflicted for the fault. The former is injustice, the latter is a due effect of justice and issues from a right intention. So it is evident that what makes a man guilty is worse than what imposes a just judgment on him through punishment.

CHRISTIAN: Since, therefore, the fault of man is a greater evil of man than its punishment, on what grounds do you call the punishment of man his supreme evil, while the fault is a greater evil, as was said?

PHILOSOPHER: If you reject our opinion in this matter I would be glad to listen to what you think the supreme evil of man must be called.

CHRISTIAN: It is surely what can make him worse, just as, inversely, it is certain that his supreme good is that by which he is made better.

PHILOSOPHER: And what, I pray, are these?

CHRISTIAN: Supreme hatred and supreme love of God through which it is clear that we displease or please him more who is called the supreme good properly and simply; and both certainly follow after this life. The more those who are tormented with perpetual and extreme punishment feel themselves punished by these, because of the very despair of relief they burn with all the greater hatred for him by whose judgment they are punished. They would never have wished this to be, for then they could at least be freed from punishment, and so they are far worse there in hating than they were here in their contempt.

The inverse happens with those who enjoy that vision of God of which the Psalmist speaks: "When your glory shall appear I shall be satisfied."[214] That is: after you have shown the majesty of your divinity to me through yourself, I will need nothing further, nor seek further. The more they love him whom they see more truly in himself, the better they become then, so that supreme love in the enjoyment of the supreme good, which is our true beatitude, is correctly to be called the supreme good of man. In fact, so great is that glory of the divine majesty that no one can catch sight of it and not be immediately blessed by the vision of it. This is why it is said, "The wicked man will be taken away lest he see the glory of God."[215] Therefore, when his faithful who loved him above all things see such blessedness as they had not been able to imagine by faith, this supreme joy of theirs will be their everlasting beatitude.

PHILOSOPHER: It seems right to me that the supreme good or the supreme evil of man be understood as that by which man is made better or worse, as you say. But if this happens in the future life, that is, if we become better or worse there than here, surely we seem to merit something more there than here. For the better or worse we become than before, we are judged

[214] Ps 17, 15 (Vulgate)
[215] See Is 26, 10.

deserving of greater reward or punishment. Now if there is also an increase of merits there so that the more we know God the more we love him, and if with the reward itself our love of God likewise grows so that we are always becoming better, surely the addition to our beatitude is so extended to infinity that it is never perfect because it is always receiving an increase.

CHRISTIAN: You do not realize that the time for meriting is only in this life, the time for rewarding in the other life; here "the time for planting," there "the time for gathering."[216] Therefore, although we become better there because of the reward for merits than we were here because of the merits, there is, however, no necessity for us to merit anything further there. We become better there than here because of the recompense for merits which we already possessed here. Although the recompense which is given for merits makes us better, it does not merit further reward but is only established to reward merits, and is not possessed to merit something further.

For example, with us, when someone receives some remuneration for friendship from a friend and on account of this he loves him more, he is not considered to merit an additional reward with his friend for this greater love which arose precisely because of a reward already given; in such a case merits would be extended to infinity. And indeed, although love is increased by the recompense of a reward by force of necessity, so that it seems to be necessary rather than voluntary, in fact there is such an affection naturally implanted in all that the very recompense of a reward carries with it a

---

[216] Eccl 3, 2.5.

certain increase of love. And it inflames us with a love of him through a certain necessity or self-love rather than through the virtue or love of the person who rewards us. If, therefore, among men a friend receives a reward from a friend and because of that reward is compelled to love more, but yet he is not said to gain further merit from this increase of love, why is it surprising if in the other life, when we love God more because of a reward we receive, we also do not convert this reward into further merit? Or finally, why may it not be granted that the glory of the divine majesty is so great that there can always be some progress in our vision of it so that the longer we gaze on it and the more fully it reveals itself to us, the more blessed it makes us? This constant increase of beatitude is surely worth more than a lesser beatitude which stays within one limit alone and which makes no further progress.

PHILOSOPHER: How, I ask, is any progress possible in this vision of God or any difference among those who have it since surely the supreme good is absolutely simple? Nothing but the whole can be seen, nor can something be seen by one which is not seen by another?

CHRISTIAN: But surely the diversity is not in the thing seen but in the manner of seeing it,[217] so that the better God is understood, the greater our beatitude is increased in the vision of him. For in understanding a soul or some spirit we do not all have an equal understanding, although such incorporeal

[217] See Boethius, *Consolation of Philosophy* 5, prose 4, tr. H. F. Stewart, p. 389.

natures are not said to have parts in the quantity of their essence. And when a body or a part of it is seen simultaneously by several people, it is seen by one better than by another, and according to some aspect of the nature of that body it is known better by one man than by the other, and is more perfectly understood. And although the same thing is understood, it is not, however, understood equally. Likewise, although in the understanding all may see the divine essence which is completely indivisible, they do not, however, have the same perception of its nature. But he communicates the knowledge of himself in a better and more perfect manner to one than to another in proportion to merits, and reveals himself more fully. It can certainly happen that while one person may know all that another knows, the former may know the individual elements better and more perfectly than the latter. And while the one may know as many things as the other, nevertheless, one may not have as much knowledge of the same things as the other, or may not know them as well.

PHILOSOPHER: Did what you call the fallen angels ever have that vision of God in which true beatitude consists; or at least did that principal angel who in comparison to the rest is granted the rank of "Light-bearer," have that vision?

CHRISTIAN: On no account must one believe that any single one of them who fell had it, and until after the fall of the others even those who did not fall did not receive this vision in recompense for their humility – the vision by which they were at once made blessed and confirmed in blessedness lest they fall again. In fact, all angels, just as all men, were created such that they could act both well and evilly. Otherwise those who did

not sin would have had no merit in their refusal to consent to
the sins of the others.

As regards the privilege of a certain excellence granted to
Lucifer, this was not done so much because of his beatitude as
for the keenness of his knowledge, that is, because he was
created superior to the others in the light of his knowledge and
keener in his understanding of the natures of things. When he
took this into consideration he was elated, puffed up with the
greatness of his knowledge by which he saw himself superior
to the others, and he presumed on greater things than he was
able to expect. That is, because he knew that he was superior to
the others, he judged that he could become equal to God and
would, like God, obtain a kingdom on his own. And so the
higher he raised himself through pride, the lower he fell
through his own fault.

PHILOSOPHER: Would you also clarify this, I pray: must this
supreme good of man, that is, the supreme love of God which
man receives from the vision of God, be called an accident of
man? And is it fitting that an accident be called the supreme
good of a substance, as if it were to be preferred to the
underlying substance?

CHRISTIAN: When you distinguish accidents and the substances
underlying them you turn to the words of philosophical
teaching and only judge of those things which are of the
earthly life not of the heavenly. Indeed, this secular and earthly
discipline was satisfied with those proofs alone which were
suited to the state of the present life and not to the quality of the
future life in which neither those words nor any human
teaching is necessary. They applied the rules of their arts when

they investigated the natures of things, but as it is written, "The one who is of the earth speaks on an earthly plane."[218] Therefore, if you strive to rise to the height of heavenly life which far surpasses every earthly discipline, do not support yourself too much on the rules of earthly philosophy by which earthly things are not yet able to be defined and understood completely, let alone heavenly things.

But there is no advantage in determining whether that love which is said to be possessed in the heavenly life, and which can only be truly known through experience of itself, is an accident or some quality since it far transcends all understanding of earthly knowledge. Moreover, what are the consequences for beatitude whether we say it is an accident or a substance or neither since, whatever we say or think it is not thereby changed nor does it diminish our beatitude. And if you would consider carefully what your philosophers have said about accidental and substantial forms you will see that it is not substantial to us since it is not in all of us, nor is it accidental since once it is present it cannot be absent. Whence, even in your view an accident is what can be present and absent; so what stops us from granting that the future love there, as well as the present love we have here, be called an accident? For although our substance is considered to be better or more worthy than any of its accidents, the supreme good of man seems not incongruously to be called that which makes man the best and most worthy by its own participation. And to speak more truly and more credibly, let us agree that God himself, who is alone properly and absolutely called the supreme good, is also the supreme good of man; as we said, it

---

[218] Jn 3, 31.

is by the participation in his vision which we enjoy that we become truly blessed. Indeed, from him whom we see in himself, his supreme love extends itself to us, and therefore he who is not from another, and makes us blessed in this way, is more correctly called the supreme good of man.

PHILOSOPHER: That opinion about the supreme good, which is not unknown to our philosophy, is surely acceptable. But if, as you say, this vision of God which makes us blessed appears to the eyes of the mind alone and not to the eyes of the body, why do you say it is necessary for the holy souls to take their bodies up again at the end as if their beatitude or glory would be increased thereby? For since, as you say, "The measure of man is also that of an angel,"[219] what benefit is there for your beatitude in the resumption of bodies – bodies which, although lacking to angels, nevertheless neither impede nor lessen their beatitude?

CHRISTIAN: Everything which God does he turns not so much to our beatitude as to his own glory, such as those things which are harmful to some people. And so Solomon says, "God created everything for his own ends, even the wicked for the evil day."[220] In fact, even the punishment of an evil person by which God punishes his iniquity commends the justice of God and so glorifies him. Therefore, although we would maintain that the resumption of bodies contributes no beatitude to the holy souls, we would not, however, consider to be superfluous that which contributes much to the praise of the divine power.

[219] Rv 21, 17 (Vulgate).
[220] Prv 16, 4.

For the more we knew them previously as weaker and subject to passion, afterwards they will demonstrate all the more clearly that God must be glorified when we shall see them whole and indissoluble in such a manner that no passion can come to us through them, and no dissolution can occur in them. And souls do seem to gain something pertaining to beatitude from this because, the more they will experience the greatness of the divine power, there is no denying that they will love him all the more and will be more blessed.

PHILOSOPHER: And I beg of you to clarify for us whether that vision of God in which beatitude consists can be increased or lessened by a difference of place, and whether it can be equally present in all places, or whether some definite place is assigned it where, for instance, it is necessary for all to reach who are to enjoy that vision?

CHRISTIAN: Those who do not doubt that God is everywhere through the magnitude of his power, but believe that all places are so present to him that he can do whatever he will in all places, and who believe that the places as well as everything in them are produced or directed by his operation, are not disturbed in any way by that question.[221] Surely, he is the one who still exists now without local position just as before time, and he must not be said to be in place who is in no wise localized, but rather he must be said to include all places in himself, even holding the heavens themselves in his palm, as it is written.[222] For he who existed before all things in no place,

[221] See Abelard, *Sic et Non* 40, eds. B. Boyer and R. McKeon, pp. 190-191 (PL 178: 1399-1400).
[222] See Is 40, 12.

afterwards did not make places for himself but for us. His beatitude can neither be lessened nor increased, nor experience any change, and he occupies no local position now just as before, and his totally simple and incorporeal eternity endures forever. Therefore, although he is in no wise localized, that is, restricted to a position in space, nonetheless, he is said to be everywhere, that is, in all places as well as surrounding all places through the power of his operation.

And indeed nothing occurs anywhere without his direction, and all places are present to him or he to them in such a manner that whatever he wills must come about there, and in this way, as was mentioned, he is said to be everywhere through the magnitude of his power. Whence he says through the Prophet, "I will fill heaven and earth."[223] And the Psalmist, considering that he could in no way escape the power of his anger, said: "Where can I go from your spirit? From your presence where can I flee? If I go up to the heavens, you are there; if I sink into the nether world you are present there, etc."[224] Moreover, just as he is said to be in all places or within all things through the operation of his power or his direction, because clearly it is necessary that all things be directed there by him, so, encompassing all places, he is said no less to surround them, that is, to have them in his power in such a manner that nothing can come about without him or without his direction.

Accordingly, since God is both within all things and outside of them by his power, as was said, and he penetrates by his own power all things no matter how solid they may be, what

---

[223] Jer 23, 24.
[224] Ps 139, 7-8.

place could stop him from being able to reveal his knowledge equally to all wherever he wills? In fact, in the same way that he is said to be in all places or above all places through power and not through local position, he can reveal his knowledge everywhere to whomever he wills. And that highest spiritual power to which all existing places are open cannot be blocked by any solidity or quality.

While the brightness of the sun so penetrates the most solid glass that it also sheds its light through it on us, and we believe that our bodies will be of such great lightness after the resurrection that, when spiritualized in some way, nothing material will be able to block them, similarly the body of the Lord which had been born with the womb closed when still mortal,[225] after the resurrection went in to the disciples "when the doors were closed,"[226] when completely immortal and impassible. Consequently, it must be believed even more that the highest vision of divine brightness cannot be impeded by any obstacle or be aided in illumination by its proximity to any place. For instance, you say that fire, which is more subtle than the other elements, cannot be sectioned off because its parts cannot be divided off by any intervening body. However, much less is a spiritual substance, which is far more subtle than any body, impeded by a corporeal obstacle.

Indeed, since the divinity is of such great subtlety that in comparison with it all other natures are considered to be corporeal and it alone in respect to others is judged to be incorporeal, how could its supreme brightness, which

---

[225] See *Sic et Non* 62, eds. B. Boyer and R. McKeon, pp. 239-241 (PL 178: 1430-1431).

[226] Jn 20, 26.

considers all things by knowing them, encounter an obstacle? And those who enjoy it, since they see him who sees all, are not ignorant of anything proper for them to know, no matter how distant it is. Otherwise, while enjoying paradise they would not contemplate the torments of hell and so love God more insofar as they would see that they have avoided the graver torments through his grace.

The Lord Jesus clearly suggests that this paradise consists everywhere in the very vision of God when, on the day his soul which suffered in the flesh descended to the depths to liberate his own from there, he said to the thief who confessed belief in him: "I assure you: this day you will be with me in paradise."[227] And, indeed, the soul of Christ was then not even outside of paradise when, as was said, he descended to the depths.

Therefore, according to our faith and clear reason, wherever a faithful soul may be, it finds God since he is present everywhere, as was said. And since no obstacle impedes it, it perseveres everywhere equally in its beatitude which we surely receive from the vision of God which he infuses into us and which we do not apprehend by our own powers. We certainly do not mount upwards to apprehend the brightness of the material sun, but it sheds its light on us for us to enjoy. Likewise, it is not so much that we approach God as that he approaches us, shining his brightness on us and the heat of his love from above, as it were. If we are said to draw near him in some way, it is never spatially since he does not reside in place, but it must be understood to come about through merits, for instance, to the extent that we become more like him in

---

[227] Lk 23, 43.

goodness or we are more in conformity with his will. And by receding from him we mean the contrary of the above. The venerable teacher Augustine, who was also most learned in your teachings, carefully clarifies this, saying, "We are near or remote from God who is everywhere, not locally but in morals."[228]

It follows that although the bodies of the saints will be of such agility after the resurrection that wherever souls will them to be they are believed to be, nonetheless, their departure will not stop the vision of God from making souls blessed. And the nature of the place will not be able to be punitive for those in whom there is nothing to be punished, just as before sin nothing could have harmed the first men. So when the holy angels who are sent to us carry out God's commands, they are not deprived or emptied of his vision by which they are blessed either by the nature of the place or by the distance. And the devils who dwell in the air and so are called the birds of heaven, although they may seem to be superior to us because of their location, must not for this reason be said to approach closer than we to God who is superior to all natures by the dignity of his own nature.

So Satan, coming among the sons of God and standing in the sight of the Lord holding conversation with him, as it is written in the Book of Job,[229] is not relieved of his misery by this so as to become more blessed. Indeed, he who was higher than the others, by falling from heaven clearly shows that the dignity of place contributes nothing to beatitude. For it is not because he comes among the sons of God, that is, among the holy angels,

---

[228] Augustine, *On Christian Doctrine* 1.10.10, tr. D. W. Robertson, p. 13.
[229] See Jb 1, 6.

and stands in the sight of God that the Lord comes into his sight so that the Lord is seen by him when he is seen by the Lord. He is like a blind person who stands among sighted people in the sun and who is not separated from them in space but in the benefit of light. For what the role of the quality of bodies is in the vision of the material sun, this is played by the quality of merits in the vision of the spiritual sun. And just as here differences among the virtues do not arise from the nature of bodies or places, so it is the same there for differences among rewards. And that vision of divine glory which makes them blessed appears all the more wonderful, the less the nature or diversity of place can impede or aid it, since he acts even in those who are not spatially separated in such a manner that he makes some blessed by illumination and others he leaves miserable in their blindness, just as in this life he does not refrain from acting by imparting his grace.

As was noted, God is said to be everywhere through power, but in such a way that he is said to be present in one place and absent from another through grace. Therefore, in whatever way the grace of divinity is said to be present or absent, to come or to go, it is not locally or corporeally, but rather it happens spiritually or through some effect of his operation. For if he were everywhere locally, where could he arrive locally or from where could he depart? But sometimes he is said to descend to us either through some gift of his grace which is granted to us, or through some manifestation in a visible sign, or when he does something out of the ordinary on earth. It is the same with the sun which is said to descend to us or to fill the world, not locally but effectively, that is, not by its local position, but by its illumination.

PHILOSOPHER: I am surprised that along with your reasons by which you try to convince me you also offer authorities from your Scriptures which, you have no doubt, have very little compelling force with me.

CHRISTIAN: As you know, my purpose was not to provide you with my own opinions but to acquaint you with the common faith or teaching of our forefathers. And so, in adducing these testimonies of our forefathers, I do not intend that you be compelled by this, but that you may understand that they are greater than my own creations.

PHILOSOPHER: I certainly do not disapprove if such was your intention. But let us hurry on now to what remains. If, as you claim, the power of the divine vision is so great that it can make souls blessed by its participation wherever they may be, why, I ask, is the kingdom of heaven particularly assigned to God and the holy souls, so that they are said to be principally in heaven, as if they were more blessed there? Even your own Christ provides such a personal example of this that he ascended bodily into heaven in the sight of his own and, as it is written, he sits there at the right hand of the Father whence he is promised to come in judgment to those meeting him in the air.[230] And so why is no region of the world allotted for the divine dwelling except heaven if, as you say, God, who exists everywhere, enjoys everywhere his own beatitude? The brightness of his vision is imparted to whomsoever he wills and wherever he wills, insofar as he wills, making them equally blessed everywhere, needing no aid, no location or

[230] See Mk 16, 19; Col 3, 1; 1 Thes 4, 17.

proximity to any place for this, but being completely self-sufficient. Since, I say, the Lord, who exists everywhere through his power and as if locating in one place the mansion of his majesty, says, "Heaven is my throne,"[231] and all the writers of the New as well as of the Old Testament allot no other part of the world for his habitation except heaven, can it not seem reasonable that the serenity of this superior place contributes something to their beatitude or to ours? Whence, according to Isaiah the light of the moon is promised to be just as the light of the sun for the fullness of this beatitude, and the light of the sun is promised to shine then with seven times its strength, and a new creation of heaven as well as of earth is promised, so that by this renewal of things our happiness might also be increased.[232]

CHRISTIAN: If you knew how to read Scripture in a prophetic spirit rather than in the manner of the Jews, and if you knew how to understand what is said of God under corporeal forms, not literally and in a material sense but mystically through allegory, you would not accept what is said as an unlettered person does.[233] Surely, if you follow this common opinion

[231] Is 66, 1.

[232] See Is 30, 26.

[233] For an excellent discussion in English of the senses of Scripture in the Middle Ages see B. Smalley, *The Study of the Bible in the Middle Ages*, 2nd ed., 1952 (Notre Dame, Indiana, 1964). In this passage it is clear that "prophetizare" means to read Scripture in its higher senses, and to read "in the manner of the Jews" means to remain on the level of the literal sense. For a discussion of the senses by a contemporary of Abelard see *The Didascalicon of Hugh of St. Victor. A Medieval Guide to the Arts*, translated from the Latin with an introduction and notes by Jerome Taylor, Records of Civilization: Sources and Studies, 64 (New York 1961), Book 4.1-5. Abelard

your understanding will not rise above the faith of those who only think of bodies or in bodily images: and you will surely fall into such great error that you will only be able to under-stand God as some corporeal thing made up of parts, as a head, hands, and feet, or as composed of the other members, particularly since the Scriptures attribute to him almost all the parts of the human body according to some analogy. For what unlettered or simple man would bear to listen to you if you announce that God has no eyes or ears or the other parts which seem to us necessary members. Surely, he will immediately object that one without eyes can never see, likewise one can neither hear nor work who lacks ears and hands.

Therefore, just as you believe that all these things which pertain to the body must be understood of God only in an allegorical sense, you should not doubt that statements about the bodily location of the divinity are to be taken in the same way. So when you hear Isaiah say: "Thus says the Lord: heaven is my throne, the earth is my footstool. What kind of house can you build for me, what is to be my resting place? My hand made all these things, etc.'"[234] just as you in no way understand him to be corporeal, so you should not understand heaven to be his corporeal seat nor the earth the corporeal foot-stool for his feet nor any local position his where he is thought to sit, any more than when his angels are called thrones [would you interpret this in a corporeal sense]. For it would be abhorrent that his majesty have some infirmity which would

himself provides an example of the approach to Scripture through a consideration of its multiple senses in his *Expositio in Hexaemeron* (PL. 178: 731-784).

[234] Is 66. 1-2.

need to be supported by a seat or a footstool. Therefore, by the terms "heaven" and "earth" in this passage, good and evil souls are distinguished as if they were higher and lower because of their merits. According to the Psalmist, good souls are likened to his temple or to heaven, "The Lord is in his holy temple; the Lord's throne is in heaven,"[235] because he presides over those who are higher in merit and dwells in them through grace as if in his own house and temple which was sanctified for him.

In truth, he tramples carnal souls who attend to earthly and low desires as a footstool under foot because those he hates he does not mercifully draw to himself, just as he presses the lost below him and by trampling grinds them and reduces the dissolute as if to dust. Therefore, when the Lord says he does not dwell in what is made by hand he is saying: I would have my excellent seat in holy souls and hold carnal and earthly men in great hatred. Why do you seek to construct for me a house of earthly materials as if I needed it, and not rather build in yourselves a spiritual house for me? Otherwise the visible temple is without significance, if there is no invisible temple. So when you hear future beatitude called either heaven or the kingdom of heaven, understand it as the sublimity of the future life rather than as the material position of heaven. It is well-known that sometimes it is even designated by the term "land" because of its stability, as well as by the term "heaven" because of its dignity. So the Psalmist says, "I believe that I shall see the bounty of the Lord in the land of the living."[236] And through Ezekiel the Lord himself promised future beatitude to his elect after the resurrection, saying: "O my people, I will open your

[235] Ps 11, 4.
[236] Ps 27, 13.

graves and will bring you out of your sepulchres. I will bring you into the land of Israel, and I will settle you upon your land."[237]

However, the ascension of our Lord Christ into the corporeal heavens bodily and visibly was not to benefit his glory in whom the fullness of divinity dwells bodily, but to benefit our faith. Therefore, he who, by going in to his disciples when the doors were closed, had first shown through his resurrection the subtlety of bodies which will be resurrected – a subtlety by which they will be able to penetrate everything – afterwards, in his ascension, showed that bodies will be so light that they will no longer be impeded from ascending anywhere by the earthly weight by which they were previously burdened, as it is written: "The corruptible body burdens the soul."[238] But wherever souls wish, they will be immediately transported there without any difficulty.

As to the mention of his ascension upwards to the right hand of the Father, just as the right hand of the Father is not understood to be corporeal, so neither is the sitting of the Father a local position. But by this the equal dignity and power of dominion with the Father is signified when he is said to have sat alongside at the right. And just as with the sitting at the right hand, the term "corporeally" cannot receive a literal interpretation, likewise with regard to what is said of his corporeal ascension, although in reality it took place in a corporeal way, however, it signifies his better ascent into the minds of the faithful. He had already clearly spoken of this ascension to Mary: "Do not touch me for I have not yet

---

[237] Ez 37, 12.14.
[238] Wis 9, 15.

ascended to my Father."[239] For then Christ was taken as in a cloud into heaven from the eyes of men to reside at the right hand of the Father. Taken from the view of the present and laborious life, he is represented in the preaching of the saints as being raised to such glory that in coruling with the Father he governs all things as well, and as coequal substance or Son he equally is Lord over all.

As to what you proposed with regard to the multiplication of the splendor of the moon or the sun, as if it would affect future beatitude in a corporeal way, this can easily be countered by the authority of the Prophet himself who said it, as well as on rational grounds. When the Lord spoke afterwards through Isaiah to Jerusalem and promised it the brightness of a future life he said:

> No longer shall the sun be your light by day, nor the brightness of the moon shine upon you; the Lord shall be your light forever, your God shall be your glory. No longer shall your sun go down, and your moon withdraw. For the Lord will be your light forever, and the days of your mourning shall be at an end. Your people shall all be just, they shall inherit the land forever, etc.[240]

What is this land which is to be inherited by those who would be just forever and is to be illumined by the presence of divine brightness as by the sun which never sets, except the eternity of future beatitude? Since this brightness is so great that it needs no aid to illumine, that sun is correctly said to lose the function of illumining further. And after we have become

[239] Jn 20, 17.
[240] Is 60, 19-21.

spiritual and no longer animal we will understand by experience the expression which was mentioned above: "the measure of man which is also that of an angel."[241] Finally, who is ignorant of the fact that when lesser lights are placed beside greater lights they are immediately darkened by the prevailing light or lose the power of illumining? And so what function of illumination could the corporeal light have there where the presence of divine brightness will so illumine the depths of darkness that it will even reveal the very counsels of hearts? The Apostle says: "Now we see indistinctly, as in a mirror; then we shall see face to face. Now I know in part; then I shall know even as I am known."[242]

Then we will know everything perfectly and most truly through the eyes of the heart just as the angels, where the functions of all the senses and of all governing bodies will cease, when God will be all in all.[243] In fact, the vision of him will so satisfy all our desires in all things that it will bestow on us through itself everything necessary for true beatitude. That vision of divine majesty will be for us an unfailing light, the highest sanctity, perpetual rest, a peace surpassing every sense, and finally, all good, total virtue, complete joy. For, when God will be all in all in this way, it is clear, as the same Apostle says, that then every principality and power will be done away with since that power alone will rule then in its own right, and will minister all goods to all the elect through the vision of his presence, as was said.[244] No longer will there be any angelic or

---

[241] See Rv 21, 17 (Vulgate).
[242] 1 Cor 13, 12. 15. 28.
[243] See 1 Cor.
[244] See Col 2, 15.

human principality over us in any service, no power will rule in any kingdom because nothing can be lacking where God will be all in all, where, since what is perfect will be present, what is partial will be done away with.

Now things can only benefit us partially; nothing is able to confer on us everything that is necessary. Whatever helps us now in regard to any doctrine or virtue or service functions imperfectly since it is God alone who is capable of all things. And so whatever functions imperfectly will cease since he, who is capable of all things, will suffice of himself. And so the future resumption there of the eyes of the body along with the other members of the body surely will not come about for the sake of their functions as if we needed them, but to glorify God, as we said before. For example, through them we will experience his power all the more to the extent that we will know that they will function better if need be, and we will see that they have attained a far stronger and better condition.

Now even if we were to interpret the increase of the light of the sun and moon literally and not only mystically, this must be referred to the glory of the creator rather than to the necessity of its function. For instance, with the aid of the heavenly lights and the transformation of the world God clearly shows us that the whole world must be changed for the better. What they had in a lesser way before was not because of the impotence of the creator but because of the demand of their mortal and infirm life which could never bear such great things nor even be worthy to use such great benefits.

Nonetheless, that the moon shines then as the sun is easily understood in a mystical sense, that is: the Church of the elect shines just as its sun, God, has unfailing light, and yet he, its sun, also transcends the light of his moon then in such a manner that in him alone is the perfection of light, which is signified by the sevenfold number.

PHILOSOPHER: As far as I can see, if these things are as you say, God, whose glory you proclaim in everything, seems to owe much to your faith. However, it now remains for you carefully to disclose what must also be thought of the lower world. For just as the supreme good of man will be more eagerly desired the more it is known, so, on the other hand, the supreme evil will be more avoided the less it is ignored.

CHRISTIAN: Indeed, in this matter there has been diversity of opinion in times past among your people as well as among ourselves.[245] Some think hell is a corporeal place under the earth which is called hell – "the lower regions" – because of its location which is below the other parts of the world. Others think hell is a punishment which is more spiritual than corporeal, so that just as by the term "heaven" which is the upper part of the world we designate the highest beatitude of souls, so by the term "hell" we designate the greatest misery which is said to lie all the lower the more it is known to be at a further distance from the highest beatitude, and seems more contrary to it. For just as what is better is said to be high because of the excellence of its dignity, so, on the other hand, what is worse is said to be the lowest because of its abjection.

The Old as well as the New Testament recount many things about the punishments of hell which seem impossible to be taken in a literal sense. What literal sense can be given to what the Lord says to Isaiah concerning the just and the impious:

---

[245] See Isidore, *Etymologies* 14.9, ed. W. M. Lindsay.

"And they shall go out and see the corpses of the men who rebelled against me. Their worm shall not die, nor their fire be extinguished." [246] What is this corporeal departure of the saints in order to see the punishment of the impious? What are these corporeal worms in the bodies of the damned, bodies which are to rise integral in all members, just as are the bodies of the saints? What will this corruption which is caused by worms be there, where the immortality of all bodies will be equally without any defect?

What literal meaning is possible for what the Lord says in the Gospel of the rich man and Lazarus who are dead, since the soul of the rich man is not able to have a corporeal tomb in hell? [247] Or what of the corporeal bosom of Abraham where it is reported that the soul of Lazarus is borne by angels? What tongue does the soul of the rich man have there, or what finger does Lazarus have, or what is this corporeal water, a drop of which can extinguish or diminish the fire of the rich man's burning tongue? So, since these things cannot literally happen in souls which are already separated from the flesh, neither can what is said elsewhere, "Bind him hand and foot and throw him out into the night to wail and grind his teeth." [248]

The Old as well as the New Testament seem to suggest that what they said of hell should be understood mystically rather than corporeally. For instance, just as the bosom of Abraham, where the soul of Lazarus is received, is to be understood as spiritual and not corporeal, so hell is to be understood as that spiritual torment where it is related that the soul of the rich

[246] Is 66, 24.
[247] See Lk 16, 19-26.
[248] Mt 22, 13.

man is buried. For, as long as souls lack bodies and occupy no place and exist by their own nature far more subtly than any body, where could they be spatially borne or moved or coerced as if into the confines of a body? Or what corporeal power of the elements, whether of fire or of the others, could touch or torment those who are without bodies? Such a possibility cannot be easily expressed in words or understood. For this reason the demons after the fall are said to be clothed in a kind of ethereal body which they received like a prison, as it were, so that they were also able to suffer corporeally.[249] Hence they were called ethereal powers because they could accomplish a great deal in the element in which they were embodied, just as men who rule over the earth are called earthly powers.

But if the Prophet is said to have understood the worms of the souls as a certain interior gnawing of their souls by which they are already tormented in their consciences by the hopelessness of forgiveness and the increase of future punishment, and afterwards as the fire by which they will be tormented in their bodies after they are taken up again, then it is easy for the spiritual as well as the corporeal torments of the damned to be defined as hell since these are referred to as the lowest or the most extreme in comparison to other punishments, whether they are said to be applied under the earth or any place else. For since it is certain that the earth is established above the waters, how can any physical fire be said to be under the earth unless indeed "under the earth" is understood as the depths of the earth beyond this surface of the earth on which we live? But again, since the number of the damned is infinite and,

---

[249] See Augustine, *De genesi ad litteram* 3.10.15, ed. J. Zycha, Corpus scriptorum ecclesiasticorum latinorum 28.1 (Vienna, 1894), p. 74.

according to the statement of Truth, the number of the elect will be small,[250] it perhaps will not be easy to accept the view that the bosom of the earth is large enough to be able to hold so many bodies. Consequently, if it seems to anyone that the power of the divine judgment is so great that it can punish whom it wills in all places equally, and that the nature of places has no bearing on punishment or glory, then I do not doubt that this opinion gains easier assent to the extent that it seems to commend the divine power more and to approach nearer to reason.

For were we to follow the common opinion of almost everyone who says that those placed in the same fire are tormented, some more, some less, in proportion to the quantity of fire, I do not see how such great moderation of the same fire by the divine power could be effected in regard to punishment. Rather, I believe that he can afflict with different torments those placed in different places, or that he wishes to punish all wherever they are with all possible torments and to turn all the elements into torments against them, as it is written, "The orb of the earth will fight for God against the insensate."[251] And in their judgment, the common faith asserts that the bodies of the blessed remain unharmed in the ethereal heaven itself where the purer the fire is, the sharper and more powerfully it burns and shines, and that this is granted them after the resurrection for their glory which our weakness could never have borne beforehand. In this way light renews healthy eyes and is a burden to unhealthy eyes.

And who does not see every day such a diversity of animal

[250] See Mt 22, 14.
[251] See Wis 5, 21 (Vulgate).

natures that what favors the life of some destroys the life of others, and because of the differing constitution of bodies, what benefits one, hinders another, both for animate and inanimate things. Men die under water, fish in air. It is known that salamanders live in fire which brings immediate destruction to other living things. Venom is the life of the serpent, the death of man; and the same things furnish a necessary diet for some living things and a death dealing diet for others. There is absolutely nothing which could be suitable to all natures. Those who came forth from the same womb, born together of the same father, never live by the same morals nor are they entertained or offended equally by the same things, and they do not suffer equally in the same heat or cold. Surely this difference in sufferings does not arise from the nature of what punishes but from the nature of those punished. So why is it surprising if the justice of the divine power should regulate the punishment of the risen bodies in proportion to the merits of each, whether they are in the same place or in different places, in such a manner that everything to do with punishment would apply equally to them wherever they are? Indeed he who confessed that he could never escape the vengeance of God, carefully noted this, saying: "Where can I go from your spirit? From your presence where can I flee? If I go up to the heavens, you are there; if I sink to the nether world, you are present there."[252]

Finally, who would think that the souls of evil men are tormented more in hell than the spiritual villains abiding in the air who bear their torments with them everywhere? At any rate it is certain that these latter deserve a greater torment the

[252] Ps 139, 7.8.

less doubt there is that they are more vile. Similarly, who would deny that the souls of wicked men, in bodies which have been taken up again, carry their torments with them even if no external torture is inflicted, no matter where they move?

Indeed, we see many sufferings of the soul while it is still in the body which are either inflicted from without or which arise from within from some disturbance or imbalance of the body, and which once had cannot be taken away by a change of place. If I may pass over other sufferings, what value towards a remedy of the pain is there in the place you put a dying person or one who is afflicted with the greatest suffering, if that suffering is in no way to be appeased through the location? Or as blessed Augustine reminds us, since at the moment of our death the suffering of death is so great in the body that on account of it the soul is forced to leave the body,[253] who would not claim that in risen and already immortal bodies the suffering by which we succumbed to death here, if it were everlasting there, would be sufficient damnation, or perhaps that it could be greater than others without the addition of any external torment? For what is more in keeping with justice than that souls take up their own bodies in torment, bodies they used evilly for pleasure? It is certain, indeed, that in the dissolution of death the suffering is so great that it is believed to be enough for the purging of any sin not deserving eternal punishment, no matter how briefly it should last. As Jerome says, this is the view of the Prophet, "The Lord will not judge twice in this matter, and there shall not arise a double affliction."[254]

[253] I am unable to find in Augustine this reference to the suffering at the moment of death.

[254] Jerome, *Commentariorum in Naum* 1.9 (PL 25: 1238c), and see Abelard, *Comm. Rom.* 2, CC.CM 11: 173.

We even read that some souls of the dead which were damned refused to be returned to the present life in order to be saved through good actions, if they would be compelled to end it again through death. We have elsewhere found this account: some souls of the saints who were dying absolutely refused, at the time of their dissolution, to go to the beatitude prepared for them because of fear of the pain until the Lord ordered them to be received by angels without suffering. From this it is clear that the suffering of death is so great that, as we said, out of fear of it some refused to return for salvation, others feared to go on to beatitude. And yet it is certain that it is in the divine power to spare from this suffering whomever it wants, as the above mentioned doctor says, claiming that John the Apostle was a stranger both to the suffering of death and the corruption of the flesh.[255] Therefore, he who can entirely suspend in death the supreme suffering of death in this way wherever and for whomever he pleases, seems to be able much more easily to inflict it wherever he wills. Surely a nature susceptible to suffer is more apt to incur suffering than to be free from it.

From this I now think it is clear to all that the location has nothing to do with the punishment of the damned just as it has nothing to do with the glory of the blessed. But to be tormented in hell or to be given over to perpetual fire is to be punished by those supreme pains which are compared particularly to fire because the torment of this element seems to be sharper. It also seems to commend the glory of the divine power in the highest way if he distributes the punishment of damnation and the

---

[255] A generally held legend whose source is unknown to me, see Abelard, Sermon 25 (pl. 178: 538c).

glory of beatitude equally in all places — he who, undoubtedly, is not absent from any place through his power.

PHILOSOPHER: As I see it, you are anxious to turn to the praise of the divine power the punishment of the damned as well as the glory of the elect, and so you proclaim his great benefits even in the greatest evils.

CHRISTIAN: And it is surely proper to do so because all his works are magnificent and full of wonder. However, I think it is unnecessary to define the places where these things may occur as long as we are able to obtain them or to avoid them.

PHILOSOPHER: And so our discussion has indeed come to this, that after the description of our supreme good as well as of our supreme evil as it appeared to you, according to our plan you should no less carefully disclose what paths lead to them so that the more we know them, the better able we will be to hold to the one or to avoid the other. But because it does not seem that what the supreme good or the supreme evil are can be satisfactorily understood yet, I wish that it be first determined how good and evil in general are to be spoken of and, if you are able, I wish you to define them. Indeed, we know many species of these, but we are not adequate to the task of understanding or stating how good or evil things are to be described. In fact, our authors who call some things good, others evil, and others indifferent, did not distinguish them by definitions but were satisfied with certain examples to illustrate them.[256]

---

[256] See Cicero, *De finibus bonorum et malorum* 3.16.53, tr. H. Rackham, Loeb Classical Library (New York, 1921); Seneca, *Ad Lucilium epistolae morales* 117.9, tr. R. M. Gummere, The Loeb Classical Library (Cambridge, Mass., 1925), vol. 3.

CHRISTIAN: I appreciate how much difficulty they thought there was in defining those things whose terms scarcely ever seem to have one single meaning. In fact, when we say "good man" or "good workman" or "good horse" or the like, who is unaware that this term "good" borrows different meanings from its adjectival position? We say a man is good for his morals, a worker for his knowledge, a horse for its strength or speed or whatever pertains to its usefulness. However, the meaning of "good" varies so greatly in its adjectival use that we do not even hesitate to link it with the terms for vices, saying for instance, a "good" or "excellent thief", since in carrying out this evil he is clever or sly. We sometimes apply the term "good" not only to things themselves but even to what is said of things, that is, to the expressions of propositions, so that we say that it is good that evil exist, although we would in no way grant that evil is good. Indeed, it is one thing to say "evil is good," which is clearly false, and another to say "it is good that evil exist," which cannot be denied. So why is it surprising that we, as they, are not able to define the various meanings which are so shifting?

Yet, as it appears to me now, I think the good in general, that is, a good thing, is said to be that which, since it is suited to some use, must not have the result of obstructing the advantage or worth of anything. On the other hand, I believe an evil thing is called that through which the opposites of these must result. I think an indifferent thing, that is, a thing neither good nor evil, is anything whose existence does not necessarily have the result of deferring or obstructing any good, such as the casual movement of a finger or similar actions. For actions are judged good or evil only on the basis of the intention which is at the root of them; but all, of themselves, are indifferent. And if we carefully examine the matter, [we see] they confer no merit and they are of themselves neither good nor evil since they pertain equally to the reprobate as well as to the elect.

PHILOSOPHER: I think we should stand here and remain for a while to see whether what you have said can perhaps stand for definitions.

CHRISTIAN: It is very difficult to circumscribe accurately everything with their proper definitions in such a manner that they can be distinguished from all other things, particularly now since we are not granted the time to think through our definitions. We learn most terms which refer to things from linguistic usage, but we are unable to mark out what they mean or how we are to understand them. We even encounter many things whose designations and meanings we are not able to encapsulate in a definition. For even if we were not ignorant of the natures of things, nonetheless, terms for them are not in use and frequently the mind is quicker to understand than the tongue to express or to discourse on what we feel. Surely, we all know from the daily use of language what things are called rocks. However, what the proper differences of a rock are or what the property of this species is, at this point I believe we would be unable to mark out in language by which some definition or description of the rock could be developed. And it ought not to seem surprising to you if you see me inadequate in matters for which we know those great teachers of yours, whom you call philosophers, were not adequate. Nonetheless, I shall try to reply what I can to the objections raised by your questions in regard to what I have proposed.

PHILOSOPHER: What you now say seems to be reasonable enough and is borne out in fact. But surely, things said are spoken in vain unless they are understood; nor can they instruct others unless they can be spoken.[257] Now, if it is agreeable – indeed because you have just consented – I wish you to provide some explanation for what you have said. When you defined a good thing why, I say, did it not seem to be enough for you to say, "what is apt for some use," that is, fit for usefulness?

CHRISTIAN: A common proverb withstands probing: "There is hardly a good that may not do harm, nor an evil that may not do some good." For example: take someone who long ago practised such good works that, being frequently praised for this, either he trusts in his own virtues and is raised to the point of pride, or another is inflamed with envy on account of this. So here it is clear that evil comes from good, and frequently good is even the cause of evil. In fact, our vices or sins, which should properly be called evils, only reside in the soul or in good creatures, and corruption cannot arise except from the good. On the other hand, who does not frequently see men arise stronger or better than they were before through humility or penance after experiencing great ruin caused by sins? Finally, it is clear that penance for sin is an evil rather than a good since it is an affliction of the mind and cannot combine with perfect beatitude since it inflicts sorrow. But no one doubts that it is necessary for the forgiveness of sins.

---

[257] Abelard records a similar remark his students made to him, see *The Story of Abelard's Adversities*, tr. J. T. Muckle, p. 39.

Who does not also realise that the supreme goodness of God, which allows nothing to come about without a reason, preordains evils so well and also uses them so optimally that it is even good that evil exist, although evil is in no way good? For just as the greatest wickedness of the devil often uses even good things in an evil way to convert them into the causes of worse effects, and in this way certain evils are done through those things which are good, so, on the contrary or conversely, God acts, making many good things to arise from evils. And he often uses in the best way the same things which the devil strives to use in the worst way. Indeed, both the tyrant and the prince can use the same sword evilly and well, the one for violence, the other for just punishment. And, I believe, there are no instruments or anything suitable for our use which we are not able to use both evilly and well through the quality of our intention. In this, what is done is not what matters, but with what mind it is done.[258] Consequently, all men, good as well as bad, are the causes of good things as well as of evil things, and through them both evil and good occur. For the good man does not seem to differ from the bad man because he does what is good, but rather because he acts well.

Although today linguistic usage makes no distinction between acting well and doing good, yet speech in its import and meaning perhaps does not signify in that way. For just as "good" is often said but not "well," that is, with a good intention, so it seems that good can be done when it is not done well. In fact, it often happens that the same thing is done by

[258] "For God thinks not of what is done but in what mind it may be done." Abelard, *Ethics*, ed. D. E. Luscombe, p. 29 with notes; see Letter 1, Heloise to Abelard, tr. B. Radice, p. 115.

different people in such a way that through their respective intentions the one does it well and the other evilly. This is the case, for example, if two men hang a criminal, the one indeed for the sole reason that he hates him, the other because he has to exercise justice.[259] Here the hanging by the latter is done justly because it is done with a right intention, but the hanging by the former is done unjustly because it is not done out of love of justice but out of zealous hatred or anger. Sometimes even bad men or the devil himself are said to cooperate with God in the same deed, so that one says that the same deed is done by God as well as by them. And consider this: what Job possessed we see taken from him by Satan, and yet Job himself declares that they were taken from him by God, saying, "The Lord gave, the Lord has taken away."[260]

From this let us come to what the minds of Christians dearly embrace, even if it seems ridiculous to you or to your like.[261] The handing over of our Lord Jesus into the hands of the Jews is reported to have been done by Jesus himself, as well as by God the Father, or by Judas the traitor. For the Father is said to have handed over the Son, and the Son is said to have given himself up, and Judas is said to have handed him over since in this either the devil or Judas did the same as God did. And so if they perhaps seem to have done something good, nonetheless they must not be said to have acted well. Or if they did or willed to happen what God wills to happen, or if they should have the same will as God in doing something, are they thereby said to act well because they do what God wills to

[259] See Abelard, *Ethics*, ed. D. E. Luscombe, p. 29.
[260] Jb 1, 21.
[261] See Abelard, *Ethics*, ed. D. E. Luscombe, p. 29; *Comm. Rom.* 1, cc.cm 11: 104.

occur, or do they thereby have a good will because they will
what God wills? Not in any way! For even if they do or will to
do what God wills to be done, nonetheless they do not do it or
will to do it because they believe God wills it to be done. Nor is
God's intention and theirs the same in the same deed; and
although they will what God wills and their will and God's can
therefore be said to be the same because they will the same
thing, nonetheless their will is evil and God's good since they
will it to occur for different reasons. Likewise, although there
may be the same action of different people because clearly they
do the same thing, nevertheless, by virtue of a difference of
intention the act of one is good and the other evil because one
does it well and the other does the same thing evilly, although
they do the same action.

And what is amazing here is that the will is even sometimes
good when someone wills evil to be done by another, because
he wills it with a good intention. For the Lord has often
decreed through the devil or a tyrant that someone afflict the
innocent or those who have not merited the affliction to purge
the sins of those who are afflicted, for instance, or to increase
their merit, or to give an example of patience to others, or for
some reasonable cause, although hidden from us. Whence, Job
reminds us that the devil did evilly what God rightfully
permitted, saying, "As it is pleasing to God so let it be."[262] By
giving thanks to him he shows that he does not doubt how
rightfully it was permitted by the Lord when he adds, "Blessed
be the name of the Lord."[263] The Third Book of Kings also
teaches that the lying spirit is sent by the Lord to deceive Ahab:

[262] See Jb 1, 21 (Vulgate).
[263] Jb 1, 21.

"For when the Lord said: Who will deceive Ahab? The lying spirit came forth and stood before the Lord and said: I will deceive him. And the Lord said to him: How? And he said: I will go forth and become a lying spirit in the mouths of all his prophets. And the Lord said: You shall succeed in deceiving him. Go forth and do this."[264] And indeed the prophet Michah, when he narrated what was revealed to him before Ahab, added, "So now, the Lord has put a lying spirit in the mouths of all these prophets of yours but the Lord has decreed evil against you."[265]

Whether the Lord permits the devil to vent his anger on the saints or on the impious, it is surely clear that he only rightfully permits what is good to be permitted, and the devil only does the evil which is good to be done, and there is a reasonable cause for why it is done although it is unknown to us. For as your great philosopher reminds us in his *Timaeus* when he shows that God does all in the most fitting manner: "Everything which is generated is generated from a necessary cause. For nothing comes about whose origin is not preceded by a cause in conformity with law and reason."[266] In this it is clearly shown that whatever things are done by whomever, since they occur through the best direction of divine providence, they proceed rationally and well in the way they do. This is so because they have a rational cause for why they are done although the person who does them might not do them rationally or well, nor in doing them attend to the reason God has.

---

[264] 1 Kgs 22, 20-22.
[265] 1 Kgs 22, 23.
[266] Plato, *Timaeus* 28a, ed. J. H. Waszink, p. 20.

Therefore, since it is clear that nothing comes about without God's permission, indeed nothing can occur if he resists or is unwilling, and since it is certain that God never permits anything without a reason and does nothing except rationally so that his permission as well as his action are reasonable, surely he is not ignorant of why they must be done even if they are evils or done evilly, since he sees why he permits each single thing to occur which does occur.[267] For it would not be good that they be permitted unless it were good that they be done; nor would he be perfectly good who would not thwart what would not be good to happen, since he is capable of doing so. Plainly he would be blameworthy if he consented to an action whose occurrence would not be good. So it is clear that whatever happens to be done or happens not to be done has a rational cause why it is done or not done. Therefore, it is good that it be done or good that it not be done even if it is not done well by him who does it, or if it is evilly not done by the one who does not do it, that is, it is omitted with an evil intention. And so it is even good that evils exist or occur although the evils themselves are in no way good.

Truth himself clearly declares this when he says: "For it is inevitable that scandals should occur. Nonetheless, woe to that man through whom scandal comes."[268] This is as if he were to say clearly: It is good and fitting to human salvation that some who have been offended or angered on my account incur scandal of soul from this, that is, damnation, so that through the wickedness of some that is done through which all may be

---

[267] See Abelard, *Sic et Non* 31, eds. B. Boyer and R. McKeon, pp. 174-180 (PL 178: 1389-1393).
    [268] Mt 18, 7.

saved, that is, whoever are predestined to be healed; but woe to him, that is, future damnation, by whose counsel or persuasion this scandal is initiated. Therefore, the scandal is evil but it is good that scandal exist. It is good that something evil exist in this way, although no evil is good.

Augustine, that great disciple of Truth, attending to this matter and considering how excellently God even orders these evils, speaks of his goodness and of the malice of the devil:

> But just as God is superlatively good as creator of good natures so he is superlatively just as regulator of evil wills. The result is that when evil wills make ill use of good natures, he himself makes a good use even of evil wills.[269]

Again, he says the same of the devil:

> And God when he created him was certainly not unaware of the hostility to good that would characterize him and foresaw the good that he himself was to bring about by using the devil's wickedness.[270]

Again, further on:

> Now God would never create any man much less any angel if he already knew that he was destined to be evil, were he not equally aware how he was to turn them to account in the interest of the good.[271]

---

[269] Augustine, *The City of God* 11.17, trs. G. G. Walsh and G. Monahan, p. 213.

[270] Ibid.

[271] Augustine, *The City of God* 11.18, trs. G. G. Walsh and G. Monahan, p. 213.

Again, in another place:

> They are good taken individually; taken as a whole, however,
> they are very good because their totality constitutes the universe
> in all its wonderful fullness.[272]

Again:

> That which is called evil, when it is regulated and put in its
> own place only enhances our admiration of the good; for we
> enjoy the good more and it is praiseworthy when evil cooperates
> with the good. For almighty God, being himself supremely
> good, would never permit the existence of anything evil among
> his works, if he were not so omnipotent and good as to be able to
> bring good even out of evil.[273]

Again:

> Nor are we to doubt that God does well even when he permits
> evil. For he does not permit this except for a just reason, and all
> that is just is indeed good. Although, therefore, what is evil or in
> so far as it is evil is not a good, nevertheless it is well that not
> only good but also evil should exist. For, were it not a good that
> evil things should also exist, the omnipotent God would most
> certainly not allow evil to be, since beyond doubt it is just as easy
> for him not to allow what he does not will, as it is for him to do
> what he wills. For he is not truly called omnipotent if he cannot
> do whatsoever he pleases, or if the power of his almighty will is
> thwarted by the will of any creature whatsoever.[274]

Now see, you have heard a clear and rational demonstration
of why it is good that evil exist, although in no way is it true

---

[272] Augustine, *Faith, Hope, and Charity* 10, tr. L. A. Arand, p. 18.
[273] Augustine, *Faith, Hope, and Charity* 11, tr. L. A. Arand, p. 18.
[274] Augustine, *Faith, Hope, and Charity* 96, tr. L. A. Arand, pp. 89-90.

that evil is good.[275] It is surely one thing to say that it is good that evil exist, another to say that evil is good. For in the one case "good" refers to an evil thing, in the other it refers to the existence of an evil thing. That is, in the first case to a thing, in the second to the occurrence of a thing. As was said, we call a thing good when, since it is suited to some use, the advantage or worth of anything must not be obstructed or even diminished on its account. It would then be necessary that a thing be obstructed or diminished if by its contrary or defect the worth or advantage necessaily would not remain. For example: life, immortality, joy, health, knowledge, chastity, are such that, since they have some worth or advantage, this clearly does not remain when their contraries supervene. Likewise, it is clear that any substances whatsoever must be said to be good things because there is no necessity that worth or advantage be obstructed on their account, since they are able to confer some degree of utility. And in the case of an evil man whose life is corrupt or whose life even causes corruption (this latter is possible without his being evil), some moral deterioration must have resulted because of him.

However, I think this is enough for the present as a description of a good thing. When, indeed, we apply the term "good" to the occurrence of things, that is, to what is said by propositions and is proposed to come about through them, for example, when we say that this is good to be or good not to be, it is as if we were to say that this is necessary to fulfill some excellent disposition of God, although that disposition may be entirely hidden from us. For it is not even good for someone to do something well if it does not conform with the divine

---

[275] See Abelard, *Ethics*, ed. D. E. Luscombe, p. 47.

ordinance to do it; rather, it is in opposition because what has no reasonable cause for being done cannot be done well. However, there is no reasonable cause why something should be done when what is directed by God would have to be interfered with if the action took place. And we are often deceived when we say that it is good for us to do this or that, which everyone judges ought to be done. But since it is not consonant with the divine ordinance, we lie through error; but, as we say, we are not guilty of a lie in thinking in this way. We also often erroneously ask for many things in our prayers which will not benefit us and which are quite properly denied to us by God because of the divine plan; he recognizes better than we what is necessary for us. Whence, the principal lesson is that of Truth which should always be said in prayer to God: "Your will be done."[276]

Unless I am mistaken, I have said enough for the present to have shown, for instance, how the term "good" must be understood when it is taken simply for a good thing, or even when it is applied to the occurrence of things or to what are expressed by propositions. If something is left in the investigation concerning the supreme good which you think should be questioned further, you are permitted to introduce it or to hurry on to what remains.[277]

[276] Mt 6, 10.
[277] "The conference of the Philosopher with the Christian ends," added in Oxford, Balliol College MS 296, fol. 189v.

Bibliography

1. Works of Abelard

Boyer, Blanche B. and Richard McKeon, eds. *Peter Abailard. Sic et Non. A Critical Edition.* Chicago, 1976-1977.

Buytaert, Eligius, ed. *Petri Abaelardi opera theologica* I. *Commentaria in Epistolam Pauli ad Romanos. Apologia contra Bernardum.* Corpus Christianorum. Continuatio Mediaevalis 11. Turnholt, 1969.

———. *Petri Abaelardi opera theologica* II. *Theologia christiana. Theologia 'Scholarium' (Recensiones breviores). Capitula haeresum Petri Abaelardi.* Corpus Christianorum. Continuatio Mediaevalis 12. Turnholt, 1969.

Gandillac, Maurice de, tr. *Œuvres choisies d'Abélard.* Paris, 1945.

Hauréau, Barthélemy. "Le poème adressé par Abélard à son fils Astralabe." *Notices et extraits des manuscrits de la Bibliothèque nationale et autres bibliothèques* 34.2 (1895) 153-187.

Luscombe, David E. *Peter Abelard's 'Ethics'.* An edition with introduction, English translation and notes. Oxford, 1971.

Migne, Jacques P., ed. *Petri Abaelardi abbatis Rugensis opera omnia.* PL. 178.

Muckle, Joseph T., ed. "Abelard's Letter of Consolation to a Friend (*Historia calamitatum*)." *Mediaeval Studies* 12 (1950) 163-213. English translation: J. T. Muckle. *The Story of Abelard's Adversities.* A translation with notes of the *Historia calamitatum.* Toronto, 1954.

———. "The Personal Letters between Abelard and Heloise." *Mediaeval Studies* 15 (1953) 47-94.

Polka, B. and B. Zelechow, eds. *Readings in Western Civilization.* Vol. I. *The Intellectual Adventure of Man to 1600.* Toronto, 1970 (a translation of the Prologue to the *Sic et Non,* pp. 102-114).

Radice, Betty, tr. *The Letters of Abelard and Heloise.* Penguin Books, 1974.

Rijk, Lambert M. De, ed. *Dialectica.* First complete edition of the Parisian manuscript. 2nd revised edition. Assen, 1970.

Thomas, Rudolf, ed. *Petrus Abaelardus. Dialogus inter Philosophum, Iudaeum et Christianum.* Textkritische Edition. Stuttgart-Bad Cannstatt, 1970.

2. *Ancient and Medieval Authors*

Alan of Lille. *De planctu naturae.* PL. 210: 429-482. English translation: Douglas M. Moffat. *The Complaint of Nature.* Yale Studies in English, 36. New York, 1908.

Anonymous. "The *Exortacio* against Peter Abelard's *Dialogus inter Philosophum, Iudaeum et Christianum.*" Ed. by Edward A. Synan. In *Essays in Honour of Anton Charles Pegis,* ed. by J. R. O'Donnell, pp. 176-192. Toronto, 1974.

Anselm of Canterbury. *Proslogion.* Ed. by F. S. Schmitt. In *S. Anselmi opera omnia,* 1. Edinburgh, 1946. English translation: Eugene R. Fairweather. *A Scholastic Miscellany: Anselm to Ockham.* The Library of Christian Classics, 10. Toronto, 1970.

――――. *Cur Deus homo.* Ed. by F. S. Schmitt. In *S. Anselmi opera omnia,* 2. Edinburgh, 1964. English translation: Eugene R. Fairweather. *A Scholastic Miscellany: Anselm to Ockham.* The Library of Christian Classics, 10. Toronto, 1970.

Aristotle. *Categories.* In *Categoriae. Editio composita,* ed. by L. Minio-Paluello. Aristoteles latinus, 1.1/5. Paris, 1961.

Athanasius. *Vita beati Antonii, interprete Evagrio.* PL. 73: 125-170. English translation: R. T. Meyer. *St. Athanasius. The Life of*

Saint Anthony. Ancient Christian Writers, 10. Westminster, Maryland, 1950.

Augustine. *De beata vita*. Ed by W. M. Green. Corpus Christianorum. Series Latina, 29. Turnholt, 1970. English translation: Ludwig Schopp. *The Happy Life*. The Fathers of the Church, 1. New York, 1948.

———. *De civitate dei libri XI-XXII*. Ed. by B. Dombart and A. Kalb. Leipzig, 1928-1929. Reissued in Corpus Christianorum. Series Latina, 48. Turnholt, 1955. English translation: Gerald G. Walsh and Grace Monahan. *The City of God*. Books VIII-XVI. The Fathers of the Church, 14. New York, 1952.

———. *De doctrina christiana*. Ed. by Joseph Martin. Corpus Christianorum. Series Latina, 32. Turnholt, 1962. English translation: D. W. Robertson Jr. *On Christian Doctrine*. The Library of Liberal Arts. Indianapolis, Indiana, 1958.

———. *Enchiridion ad Laurentium de fide et spe et caritate*. Ed. by E. Evans. Corpus Christianorum. Series Latina, 46. Turnholt, 1969. English translation: Louis A. Arand. *St. Augustine. Faith, Hope, and Charity*. Ancient Christian Writers, 3. Westminster, Maryland, 1947.

———. *De Genesi ad litteram*. Ed. by Joseph Zycha. Corpus scriptorum ecclesiasticorum latinorum, 28.1. Vienna, 1894.

———. *Questionum evangeliorum libri duo*. PL. 35: 1321-1364.

———. *De ordine*. Ed. by W. M. Green. Corpus Christianorum. Series Latina, 29. Turnholt, 1970. English translation: Robert P. Russell. *Divine Providence and the Problem of Evil*. The Fathers of the Church, 1. New York, 1948.

———. *In Epistolam Ioannis ad Parthos tractatus decem*. PL. 35: 1977-2062. English translation: H. Browne, revised by Joseph H. Myers. *Ten Homilies on the First Epistle of John*. Nicene and Post-Nicene Fathers, First series, 7. New York, 1888.

———. *In Iohannis Evangelium tractatus CXXIV*. Ed. by D. R. Willems following the Maurist edition. Corpus Christianorum. Series Latina, 36. Turnholt, 1954. English translation: John

Gibb and J. Innes. *Lectures or Tractates on the Gospel according to St. John.* Nicene and Post-Nicene Fathers, First series 7. New York, 1888.

[Pseudo-]Augustine. *Tractatus de oratione et eleemosyna.* PL 40: 1225-1228.

Bernard, St. Letter 190 to Innocent II. PL 182: 1053-1072. English translation: Ailbe J. Luddy. *The Case of Peter Abelard*, pp. 58-94. Westminster, Maryland, 1947.

Boethius. *De differentiis topicis.* PL 64: 1173-1216.

———. *De divisione.* PL 64: 875-892.

———. *In Categorias.* PL 64: 159-294.

———. *In Topica Ciceronis.* PL 64: 1039-1174.

———. *The Theological Tractates. The Consolation of Philosophy.* Trans. by H. F. Stewart and E. K. Rand. The Loeb Classical Library. Cambridge, Mass., 1962.

Cicero. *De finibus bonorum et malorum.* Trans. by H. Rackham. The Loeb Classical Library. New York, 1914.

———. *Ad C. Herennium. De ratione dicendi (Rhetorica ad Herennium).* Trans. by H. Caplan. The Loeb Classical Library. Cambridge, Mass., 1954.

———. *De inventione. De optimo genere oratorum. Topica.* Trans. by H. M. Hubbell. The Loeb Classical Library. Cambridge, Mass., 1949.

———. *De officiis.* Trans. by W. Miller. The Loeb Classical Library. Cambridge, Mass., 1913.

———. *Paradoxa stoicorum.* Trans. by H. Rackham. The Loeb Classical Library. Cambridge, Mass., 1942.

Epicurus. "Letter to Menoeceus." Trans. by C. Bailey. In *The Stoic and Epicurean Philosophers*, ed. by Whitney J. Oates. The Modern Library. New York, 1940.

Gregory the Great. *Homiliae XL in Evangelia.* PL 76: 1075-1312.

Honorius of Autun. *Libellus octo quaestionum. De angelis et homine.* PL 172: 1185-1192.

Horace. *The Satires and Epistles of Horace.* Trans. by S. P. Bovie. Chicago, 1959.

Hugh of St. Victor. *Hugonis de Sancto Victore Didascalion de studio legendi.* Ed. by C. H. Buttimer. Studies in Medieval and Renaissance Latin, 10. Washington, D.C., 1939. English translation: *The Didascalicon of Hugh of St. Victor. A Mediaeval Guide to the Arts.* Translated from the Latin with an introduction and notes, Jerome Taylor. Records of Civilization: Sources and Studies, 64. New York, 1961.

――. *De sacramentis christianae fidei.* PL 176: 173-618. English translation: Roy J. Deferrari. *On the Sacraments of the Christian Faith.* Cambridge, Mass., 1951.

Innocent II, Pope. *Epistolae et privilegia.* PL 179: 53-658.

Isidore. *Isidori Hispalensis episcopi Etymologiarum sive originum libri XX.* Ed. by W. M. Lindsay. 2 vols. Oxford, 1911.

Jerome. *Commentariorum in Naum Prophetam liber unus.* PL 25: 1231-1272.

――. *Contra Vigilantium liber unus.* PL 23: 353-368.

John Scottus Eriugena. *Periphyseon (De divisione naturae) liber primus.* Ed. and trans. by I. P. Sheldon-Williams with the collaboration of Ludwig Bieler. Scriptores latini Hiberniae, 7. Dublin, 1968.

Judah Halevi. *The Kuzari (Kitab al Khazari).* Translated from the Arabic by Hartwig Hirschfeld, 1905. Introduction by Henry Slonimsky. New York, 1964.

Lucan. *The Civil War.* Trans. by J. D. Duff. The Loeb Classical Library. Cambridge, Mass., 1928.

Macrobius. *Ambrosii Theodosii Macrobii Commentarii in Somnium Scipionis.* Ed. by I. Willis. Academia scientiarum Germanica Berolinensis. Bibliotheca scriptorum Graecorum et Romanorum Teubneriana. Leipzig, 1963. English translation: *Macrobius. Commentary on the Dream of Scipio.* Translated with an Introduction and Notes by William H. Stahl. Records of Civilization: Sources and Studies, 48. New York, 1952.

Ovid. *Amores*. Trans. by G. Showerman. The Loeb Classical Library. Cambridge, Mass., 1921.

Peter the Venerable. *The Letters of Peter the Venerable*. Ed. by Giles Constable. 2 vols. Cambridge, Mass., 1967.

Plato. *Timaeus a Calcidio translatus commentarioque instructus*. Ed. by J. H. Waszink. Corpus Platonicorum Medii Aevi, Plato Latinus, 4. London, 1962.

Richard Fishacre. "The Science of Theology according to Richard Fishacre: Edition of the Prologue to his *Commentary on the Sentences*." Ed. by James Long. *Mediaeval Studies* 34 (1972) 71-98.

Sallust. Trans. by J. C. Rolfe. The Loeb Classical Library. Cambridge, Mass., rev. ed., 1931.

Seneca. *Seneca ad Lucilium epistolae morales*. Trans. by R. M. Gummere. The Loeb Classical Library, 3 vols. Cambridge, Mass., 1917-1925.

Talmud. *The Babylonian Talmud. Seder Nezikin in Four Volumes*. Ed. by Rabbi I. Epstein. London, 1935.

Valerius Maximus. *Valerii Maximi factorum et dictorum memorabilium libri novem*. Ed. by C. Kempf. Bibliotheca scriptorum Graecorum et Romanorum Teubneriana. Scriptores Romani. 2nd ed. Leipzig, 1888.

William of Conches. *Das Moralium dogma philosophorum des Guillaume de Conches lateinisch, altfranzösisch und mittelniederfränkisch*. Ed. by John Holmberg. Uppsala, 1929.

3. Modern Authors

Baron, Roger. "À propos des ramifications des vertus au xiie siècle." *Recherches de théologie ancienne et médiévale* 23 (1956) 19-39.

Baron, Salo W. *A Social and Religious History of the Jews*. Vol. IV. *Meeting of East and West*. 2nd rev. ed. New York, 1957.

Benton, John F. "Philology's Search for Abelard in the *Metamorphosis Goliae*." *Speculum* 50 (1975) 199-217.

——. "Fraud, Fiction and Borrowing in the Correspondence of Abelard and Heloise." *Pierre Abélard – Pierre le Vénérable*, ed. by René Louis, pp. 469-506.

Benton, John F. and Fiorella Prosperetti Ercoli. "The Style of the *Historia calamitatum*: A Preliminary Test of the Authenticity of the Correspondence Attributed to Abelard and Heloise." *Viator* 6 (1975) 59-86.

Bird, Otto. "The Tradition of the Logical Topics: Aristotle to Ockham." *Journal of the History of Ideas* 23 (1962) 307-323.

Blumenkranz, Bernhard. *Les auteurs chrétiens latins du moyen âge sur les Juifs et le judaïsme*. École Pratique des Hautes Études-Sorbonne. Sixième section: Sciences économiques et sociales. Études Juives, 4. Paris, 1963.

Buytaert, Eligius. "Abelard's *Collationes*." *Antonianum* 44 (1969) 18-39.

——. Ed. *Peter Abelard*. Proceedings of the International Conference, in Mediaevalia Lovaniensia, Series I/Studia II. Louvain, 1974.

Chenu, Marie-Dominique. "Notes de lexicographie philosophique médiévale: 'Disciplina'." *Revue des sciences philosophiques et théologiques* 25 (1936) 686-692.

——. *La Parole de Dieu* I. *La foi dans l'intelligence*. Paris, 1964.

——. *Nature, Man, and Society in the Twelfth Century. Essays on New Theological Perspectives in the Latin West*. Selected, edited, and translated by Jerome Taylor and Lester K. Little. Chicago, 1968. (An English translation of selected chapters from *La théologie au douzième siècle*. Paris, 1957.)

Engels, L. "Abélard écrivain." *Peter Abelard*, ed. by E. M. Buytaert, pp. 12-37.

Graboïs, Aryeh. "The *Hebraica Veritas* and Jewish-Christian Intellectual Relations in the Twelfth Century." *Speculum* 50 (1975) 613-634.

——. "Un chapitre de tolérance intellectuelle dans la société occidentale au XIIe siècle: le *Dialogus* de Pierre Abélard et le

Kuzari d'Yehudah Halévi." In *Pierre Abélard – Pierre le Vénérable*, ed. by R. Louis, pp. 641-652.

Häring, Nikolaus M. "Abelard Yesterday and Today." In *Pierre Abélard – Pierre le Vénérable*, ed. by R. Louis, pp. 341-403.

Haskins, Charles H. *The Renaissance of the Twelfth Century*. Cambridge, Mass., 1927.

Jolivet, Jean. "Abélard et le philosophe (Occident et Islam au xiie siècle)." *Revue de l'histoire des religions* 164 (1963) 181-189.

Kurdziałek, M. "Beurteilung der Philosophie im *Dialogus inter Philosophum, Iudaeum et Christianum*. In *Peter Abelard*, ed. by E. Buytaert, pp. 85-98.

Liebeschütz, H. "The Significance of Judaism in Peter Abaelard's *Dialogus*." *Journal of Jewish Studies* 12 (1961) 1-18.

Louis, René, ed. *Pierre Abélard – Pierre le Vénérable. Les courants philosophiques, littéraires et artistiques en Occident au milieu du xiie siècle*. Colloques internationaux du Centre national de la recherche scientifique, no. 546, Paris, 1975.

Luscombe, David E. "Nature in the Thought of Peter Abelard." *La filosofia della natura nel medioevo*, pp. 314-319. Atti del terzo congresso internazionale di filosofia medioevale. Milan, 1966.

——. *The School of Peter Abelard. The Influence of Abelard's Thought in the Early Scholastic Period*. Cambridge Studies in Medieval Life and Thought, n.s. 14. Cambridge, 1969.

——. "The *Ethics* of Abelard. Some Further Considerations." In *Peter Abelard*, ed. by E. Buytaert, pp. 65-84.

Monfrin, Jacques. "Le problème de l'authenticité de la correspondance d'Abélard et d'Héloïse." In *Pierre Abélard – Pierre le Vénérable*, ed. by R. Louis, pp. 409-424.

Roques, R. "Les *pagani* dans le *Cur Deus homo* de Saint Anselm." In *Miscellanea Mediaevalia*. Bd. 2. *Die Metaphysik im Mittelalter. Ihr Ursprung und ihre Bedeutung*, ed. by Paul Wilpert, pp. 192-206. Vorträge des ii. internationalen Kongresses für mittelalterliche Philosophie. Berlin, 1963.

Sikes, Jeffrey G. *Peter Abailard*. Cambridge, 1932.

Smalley, Beryl. *The Study of the Bible in the Middle Ages.* 2nd rev. ed., 1952. Notre Dame, Indiana, 1964.

Thomas, Rudolf. *Der philosophisch-theologische Erkenntnisweg Peter Abaelards im 'Dialogus inter Philosophum, Iudaeum et Christianum'.* Untersuchungen zur allgemeinen Religionsgeschichte. Neue Folge, 6. Bonn, 1966.

——. "Die Persönlichkeit Peter Abaelards im *Dialogus inter Philosophum, Iudaeum et Christianum* und in den *Epistolae* des Petrus Venerabilis: Widerspruch oder Übereinstimmung?" In *Pierre Abélard – Pierre le Vénérable,* ed. by R. Louis, pp. 255-269.

Williams, A. Lukyn. *'Adversus Judaeos'. A Bird's-Eye View of Christian 'Apologiae' until the Renaissance.* Cambridge, 1935.

Index of Biblical References

Index of Authors and Names

(Latin titles are given for the works of Abelard, Augustine, Boethius, and Cicero. English titles are added for existing translations.)

Index of Subjects